LITTLE GIRLS

1

ELENA GIANINI BELOTTI

Little Girls

Social conditioning and its effects on the
stereotyped rôle of women during infancy

Writers and Readers

Writers and Readers Publishing Cooperative Ltd.
25 Nassington Road London NW3
Dalla parte delle bambine first published 1973 by
Giangiacomo Feltrinelli Editore Milan Italy
This translation published by Writers and Readers
Publishing Cooperative 1975. Reprinted 1981.

This book was translated and produced collectively by
Lisa Appignanesi, Amelia Fletcher, Toshiko Shimura,
Sian Williams and Jeanne Wordsworth.

Printed in Canada by the Hunter Rose Co. Ltd., Toronto.

SBN 0 904613 07 0

CONTENTS

It ought to be impossible to read this book without asking one-self some searching questions about one's own upbringing, or about the way one brings up one's own children. Simply written, easy to read, and clearly argued, it states that discrimination against women begins in the cradle; or earlier, in the womb. Naturally, the argument will enrage a great many people, not least those who firmly believe that they at least are free from prejudice and dis-crimination. Many parents, reading these pages, will say as I did, 'Well, of course *I* wouldn't treat my children like that' – only to reflect, if they are honest, that perhaps after all there are areas in which they are guilty of quite unthinking, heavily pre-conditioned, responses.

Few liberated parents would admit to some of the grosser of the attitudes described by Elena Belotti, though they would admit that of course 'other people' have them. Who would dare to blame a wife for producing nothing but daughters, knowing, as we know these days, that the man decides the child's sex? And yet has not this very knowledge brought in an equally sexist and irrational fear – that a man who produces nothing but daughters is in some way less 'virile' than a father of five boys? Few of us would admit that we think our daughters' education less important than our sons', despite the evidence in statistics of University places, fee-paying schools, and so on. Equally, few would admit that they feel uneasy when watching their boys choose stereotyped 'female' tasks or games. But even the most advanced amongst us shrink, ridicu-lously, from dressing baby boys in pink. And when Ms. Belotti says that most parents would put their foot down if a girl de-manded a toy machine gun as a birthday present, or a boy a toy tea set, is she right or wrong?

Her book coolly and wittily peels off the layers of prejudice and preconception which clothe all of us. Her observations are acute: her detail excellent. She is a woman who knows and has worked with children for years, and her case histories, of Laura, Alessia, Betta, Giorgetto are full of affectionate, amused attention. Her respect for the autonomy, courage and sheer enterprise of very small children is something that any parent will admire: she sees them not as helpless little creatures, in constant need of protection, but as battlers for freedom and learning, sometimes tragically crushed in an uneven struggle. She also knows nursery school teachers and mothers (significantly, there are few mentions of real fathers – evidently they do not visit the nursery schools), and some of their case histories, which ring all too true, remind one more of the sadism Charlotte Brontë describes in *Jane Eyre* than of the enlightened child-oriented twentieth century. Reaction and cruelty flourish in nursery and infant schools: her realistic account is worth more than many well-intentioned platitudes about vocation and aptitude. She is a writer who knows her material thoroughly, and who has good cause to protest against the quite unnecessary hardships imposed upon small children. She recounts some extreme cases, but also cares for the thousand little subtle manoeuvres by which luckier or more submissive little girls manage to avoid becoming extreme cases. Her argument, as a whole, is overwhelmingly proven.

This does not mean that I agree with every detail of it. One of the interests of the book is the constant questioning that it arouses. For instance, it is clear that as her book was written in Italy, for Italians (and was an immense best-seller), it will have a different emphasis from a book written in an English context. As she herself points out, one of the reasons why girls are so undervalued is because of their low economic potential in a peasant economy, and, as England has been industrialised longer than any other European country, one would expect to find a certain shift in the evaluation. Not a dramatic one, but a small one. And personally, I think it exists: there has been a long and honourable tradition of feminism and protest in this country, a Protestant tradition, which has enabled women to speak out more than they have been able to do in a basically Catholic, less industrial society. So, at times, from our point of view, she exaggerates. More fascinating, she reveals what seem to me certain national differences of outlook on sexuality: she states that whereas little girls in Italy are taught to be modest and dress themselves politely, nobody minds if little boys run around naked, expose themselves, and play with their genitals. I would be surprised if this were generally true in England: it is as least as common to see naked little girls on an English beach as naked boys, if not more common, and I would have thought it possible that the English, for reasons good or bad, reprimand male masturbation at least as strongly as female, probably more strongly,

The English nanny threatening the little boy that she will cut it off if he plays with it is as real an ogre as those described by Ms. Belotti. Little girls, having nothing to lose, are spared at least that threat. (She is good, though, at demolishing the theory of penis envy: 'No woman,' she says, 'except for so-called "deviants", seriously wishes to be male and have a penis. But most women would like to have the privileges and the opportunities that go with it.')

I would also query her view (or, rather, the views of Brunet and Lézine) on mothers' attitudes to breast-feeding boys or girls. She states that mothers prefer to suckle boys, pay them more attention, suckle them for longer, and object less to their greed. Without any statistical support, I would be surprised if this were not less true in England, and quote a letter in support (admittedly a very small statistic, but published in that not-very-avant-garde paper, the *Evening News*), which claims:

THE PLEASURE and satisfaction of breast feeding far outweigh any discomfort felt in the early days after birth. The feel of a little head and body snuggling against one's breast is marvellous. I was only sorry to give it up when my son was seven months old, as I was pregnant again, and at 13 months with my daughter; her teeth were rather sharp. – Maureen Collins, Gordon House Road, N.W.5.

In my experience, it is very rare for mothers to discriminate amongst their babies at this stage on grounds of sex: it is true that a whole host of old wives' tales surround the mystery of feeding and baby behaviour, but most mothers are observant and realistic enough to notice that all babies behave in a thoroughly individual way, as far as feeding, crying, vomiting, etc. go, and that there is little to be gained from expecting a stereotyped sex response from a three-month-old infant. Perhaps child-rearing patterns are more old-fashioned in Italy: one was alarmed to read of mothers seriously attempting to pot-train babies from birth. (There are other evidently Italian customs in the text: it is surely not very common for women in England to visit shrines in order to be blessed with a son, though there may be other quaint English customs of the same nature that a folk-lorist could uncover.)

But Ms. Belotti's descriptions of play patterns amongst children have a universal, international validity, and her explanation for the female passion for skipping and ball-bouncing is as convincing as her observations are acute and first-hand. Her confident dismissal of Erikson's 'internal space' interpretation of little girls' artistic creations is as challenging as her attack on Freud. Reading the descriptions of subtly manipulated class-room play, most adults will be able to supply illustrations from their own experience – a suppressed desire to play at wash-day or shopping, to join in the cricket or football. Perhaps girls will even question why it is that they never had the slightest interest in anything mechanical, and regarded the boyish ambition of traindriving with complete apathy. Which explanation is more plausible, the Freudian–Eriksonian one, or the environmental–opportunity one provided by this book? No one theory can cover every case, and some girls are brought up in households where cars, engines and football are part of daily life: equally, some boys never have the slightest interest in them. But overall, Elena Belotti is persuasive. A constant, steady, subconscious, unarticulated pressure from birth is strong enough to dissuade all but the most energetic or gifted from wanting to do anything. The lack of positive female images in children's fiction is well illustrated: interestingly, one of the fairy stories chosen for attack. *The Fisherman's Wife*, is used by Virginia Woolf in *To The Lighthouse* in her extraordinarily delicate and ambiguous counter-balancing of Mrs. Ramsay, Mr. Ramsay, and their son. The Freudian interpretation of *Little Red Riding Hood* may well be more complex, but it is not likely to be as amusing or as trenchant as this one. Little girls in children's books smile: little boys are allowed to sulk. The morals drawn from this are interesting, and convincing.

It struck me that there was one anomaly in the account of children's fiction. The book quotes from an enquiry by Michèle de Wilde into female stereotypes in French and American children's books: both seem to agree that such books rarely describe girls who are good at skating or riding. This description could hardly be applied to English fiction: the *genre* may be dying out, but certainly some years ago there was a vast amount of literature written for girls about horses, much of which is still popular. Is the Freudian explanation here more valid? Why do little English girls have such a passion for horses, and why is such a mystique attached to them? There has, of course, been for a long time a sub-current in England praising the 'tomboy' girl: Maggie Tulliver, certainly a heroine and a popular one, was one of its first exemplars, but she was followed on a much more popular level by plenty of boyish heroines. Arthur Ransome's *Swallows and Amazons* series offers a fascinating array of stereotypes: the mother of the family stays at home while father is at sea. Susan is 'the little mother' of all the children's expeditions, and yet she in turn is off-set by the daring, expert, boyish professional sailors, Nancy and Peggy, who despise girlish names, and challenge the boys to physical combat. Perhaps outdoor, sporty, horsey women have always been more numerous in England than on the Continent and in the United States: certainly here there has always been a tradition of women riding to hounds, and it is not surprising that this tradition has found admirers amongst girls who have never been near a hunt, and have paid only occasional visits to riding stables. Perhaps the popularity of horse books supports Elena Belotti's point. Once an energetic, competitive outdoor sport is given the seal of approval, thousands of frustrated indoor children, fed up with the non-glamorous inactivity of embroidery and house-keeping, will rush to approve it, and to read about it even if they are too poor or too urban to practise it.

I hope it is evident from what I've said that even where I do not wholly agree with Elena Belotti, I find her arguments well-made and provocative. Nobody could read this book without making some radical re-appraisals. Personally, for a long time after I'd finished it, I was constantly checking up on my own behaviour, and that of other parents – was it true that mothers always asked a daughter to help with the supper, never a son? Did one let the boys mess their bedrooms up more than the girls? Underneath the ragged-trousered appearance of one's daughters, were there really suppressions and hesitations? I am sure there has been change and progress, in recent years: little boys, and even big boys, now cry in public much more freely than they used to, little girls are more assertive, physically more courageous. And it is not desirable to become too aware, too much of the time, of one's sexist assumptions: one undesirable side-effect from reading the book was my own doubt that there might be something *wrong* with my boys because their handwriting, unlike Belotti's stereotype, is so readable and tidy, and something *wrong* with my girl, because hers is such a frightful unfeminine mess – a point which had certainly not crossed my mind before. One cannot constantly think in terms of right and wrong, male and female: as Virginia Woolf said, [in *A Room of One's Own*] too much dwelling upon differences 'disturbs the unity of the mind'. But, in the present state of society, one has to dwell upon them some of the time. As she also said. Elena Belotti is right to go to the root of the matter, to the conditioning of the earliest years, and her book, fortunately, is written in language plain enough to get its message across to mothers, fathers and nursery school teachers, as well as to the sophisticated professional educators and theorists. I hope it will be read by those mothers who can still be overheard saying, 'One good thing about little girls, at least you can dress them up', by those fathers who try to force shy or unaggressive boys into aggressive sports and who sneer at the thought of their being taught to sew on buttons. Whatever one's views on the essential or innate differences between the sexes (and there may be more than this book allows, I feel), no reasonable person can think it unmanly to sew on buttons, unwomanly to become a mathematician. And yet these are, still, the assumptions of our society. They reveal a great terror: of woman, of the undifferentiated mass, of sex itself, of loss of male power. It is only by understanding the terror that we can give all children, as individuals, a chance of happiness. This book is a plea that we should think about what we are doing, rather than blindly perpetuate the mistakes of our mothers and fathers, and it deserves to be treated with the greatest seriousness. No power on earth will ever be strong enough to prevent parents from wanting children of both sexes, and society will have to reform itself out of recognition before men cease to want 'a son and heir' as well as daughters, before women cease secretly and irrationally to congratulate themselves upon producing one; but that is no excuse for treating little girls as second-class citizens. Nobody could deny, after reading this book, that in most households they are so treated. The remedy, for once, really does begin at home.

Margaret Drabble, June 1975

In his book, *The Subjection of Women*, written in 1869, John Stuart Mill first questions the concept of a 'feminine nature'. Up until then, this concept had permitted reference to a series of characteristics supposedly particular to woman. Mill, however, demonstrated that these characteristics were the logical product of a precise historical, social and cultural context. In this lucid and passionate defence of woman, Mill used psychology to analyse

> ... the laws of the influence of circumstances on character. ... The profoundest knowledge of the laws of the formation of character is indispensable to entitle anyone to affirm even that there is any difference, much more what the difference is, between the two sexes considered as moral and rational beings. ... [1]

Mill analyses the influence of education. He furthermore indicates the most certain and simple path towards a knowledge of woman which is not merely – as is often the case – the reflection of the vision that man has of her. He addresses himself directly to the interested party and makes subtle observations concerning the conditions necessary for woman to be able to speak about herself, describe herself, expose herself without feeling subordinate to man. There can be no authentic dialogue between persons caught in a relationship of dominating and dominated. On the contrary, for dialogue to exist the persons concerned must see themselves as equals. Thus to hear what woman has to say, man must experience her as an equal. But if men were merely to *listen* to what women have to say about themselves, a large proportion of the problems which exist between the sexes would immediately disappear. This is far from being the case at the moment.

Every woman who proposes to speak about herself and her cultural rôle can tell the tale of her girlhood, adolescence and young womanhood, as well as narrate the experiences she believes to have been caused by her sex. But no matter how far she pushes her self-analysis, she always discovers a hidden region of which she can say nothing. This is the obscure zone of infancy which lies at the basis of all subsequent difficulties. By the age of three or four – that is, as far back as an individual's memory can carry him – everything in a person's destiny which is linked to his sex is already determined. This is due to the fact that during this early period there can be no conscious struggle against oppression.

Our individuality has profound roots which escape us because they do not belong to us. Without our knowledge, others have cultivated them for us. The little girl, who at the age of four is entranced by her own mirror image, is already conditioned to this kind of contemplation by her four previous years, not to mention her nine months in utero during which all the elements which were to make her a woman, as similar as possible to all other women, came into play.

Like all other cultures, our own uses the various means at its disposal to obtain from both male and female those patterns of behaviour which are most appropriate to the values the culture finds it important to preserve and transmit. The goal of identifying the child with the sex which is assigned to it is quickly attained. Yet there is no element which permits us to deduce that this complex phenomenon of sexual identification has any biological roots.

> . . . Despite the existence of hormonal and genetic factors, it is education which acts as the decisive element in sexual identification and determines whether one considers oneself to be boy or girl. The results of research done on children whose sexual development is defective lead one to believe that identification with one sex or the other, as well as the assuming of a determined sexual rôle, essentially takes place through apprenticeship.[2]

This book finds its starting point in direct observation of the child from his moment of birth. It then analyses the behaviour of adults towards the child; the relations they establish with him throughout his growth; the types of demands made of him and the way in which they are made; and everything that is expected of him depending on his sex. It further looks at the efforts the child has to make to adapt himself to adult demands and expectations; the rewards or rejections which face him depending on whether he submits to sexual stereotyping or not. The research has been carried out in crèches, nursery, primary and secondary schools.

No proof exists to support the hypothesis which states that the different behaviour of the sexes is innate. In this respect, the opposite hypothesis – which considers behaviour to be the result of the social and cultural conditioning to which children are subjected from their birth – remains just as viable. But although biology and psychology are both unable to tell us exactly what is innate and what is learned, anthropology does give us precise answers which support the second hypothesis. No one can modify innate biological conditions (given that these exist). But it is possible to modify such social and cultural conditions as might be at the basis of the difference between the sexes. Before trying to change these conditions, however, it is necessary to know them. Their genesis lies in those little daily gestures which generally pass unnoticed, those automatic reactions whose reasons and ends escape us. We repeat these without being aware of their significance, because we have interiorised them through the educational process. The origins of these conditions are further visible in prejudices which can be accounted for neither by reason nor by the passage of time, but which we nevertheless continue to see as intangible truths; and finally in customs based on an extremely rigid code of rules. It is not easy to break a chain of conditioning which is linked almost invisibly from one generation to another. But there are historical moments in which breaks in the chain can more easily be made than in others. Today, for example, when all the values of our society are going through a crisis phase, the myth of the male's 'natural' superiority and the female's 'natural' inferiority has been shaken.

> The traditional superiority of adults over children is rapidly in the process of disappearing. At the same time male superiority, the supremacy of the white race, and the power of capital over labour are crumbling.[3]

In the following analysis, the critique made of women is not intended as an act of accusation. Rather it is meant as a spur towards consciousness: consciousness of the conditioning women undergo, so that this will not be reproduced, and an awareness that the situation can be changed.

The break which must be made with the past is one which concerns everyone and especially those women to whom the education of children is confided. This rupture does not consist in shaping little girls into a masculine mould, but in assuring that each individual is given the possibility of developing in whatever way suits him best, independently of the sex to which he belongs. If what we examine here is the little girl's case, it yet remains quite clear that girls are not the only victims of a negative conditioning based on sex.

According to Margaret Mead:

> All discussion of the position of women, of the character and temperament of women, the enslavement and the emancipation of women, obscures the basic issue – the recognition that the cultural plot behind human relations is the way in which the rôles of the two sexes are conceived, and that the growing boy is shaped to a local and special emphasis as inexorably as is the growing girl.[4]

What can a boy gain that is positive from the arrogant presumption that he belongs to a superior caste merely because he was born a boy. The mutilation which he undergoes is just as catastrophic as that of the girl who is persuaded of her inferiority by the very fact that she is female. The boy's development as an individual is deformed, his personality impoverished, and this makes relations between the sexes difficult.

No one can say how much energy and how many qualities are destroyed in the process of forced integration of children of both sexes into the preconceived masculine and feminine moulds of our culture. No one will ever be able to tell us what could happen to a girl if she did not find quite so many insurmountable obstacles placed in the path of her development, solely because of her sex.

Legal equality, equal wages, access to all possible professions, are sacrosanct objectives which have been offered to women – at least on paper – at the moment when men have deemed it right. These rights will, however, remain inaccessible to most women until such a time as the psychological structures which prevent them from wanting and being able to appropriate these rights are modified. It is these psychological structures which taint all woman's attempts to fit into the world of production with guilt; which make her feel she has failed as a woman if she does enter this world, or alternately failed as an individual, if she chooses to realise herself as a woman. The need to realise and affirm oneself as an individual, the desire for autonomy and independence which women are reproached for lacking, have already been severely shaken in a woman by the time the fundamental choices of adolescence have to be made.

Notes*

1 John Stuart Mill, *The Subjection of Women*, Everyman Library, London 1929, p. 240.
2 Carl Fred Broderick, *Individual Sex and Society*, John Hopkins University Press, Baltimore 1969.
3 Rudolf Dreikurs, *Psicologia in classe*, Giunti, Florence 1967, p. 7.
4 Margaret Mead, *Sex and Temperament*, Routledge & Kegan Paul, London 1935.

  * Wherever possible, the English edition has been quoted, but in some cases translation has been made from the Italian edition.

CHAPTER 1

EXPECTING THE BABY

> *'Quello che gli pende lo difende'*
> *Popular saying*
> (*Upon him hangs the part*
> *which he defends with all his heart.*)

A child's sex is determined by its father. There are two kinds of spermatozoa: those bearing X chromosomes which produce females, and those bearing Y chromosomes which produce males. Current scientific knowledge tells us that it is purely a matter of chance whether the female ovum is fertilised by a sperm bearing an X chromosome or a sperm bearing a Y chromosome. But in spite of science's certainty that the father is responsible for determining the sex of the foetus, the idea seems to have some difficulty in taking root. It conflicts with the opposing and deeply ingrained prejudice which makes the woman responsible for the sex of the child, whether for good or ill.

'My wife has given me a fine boy.' 'My wife can't produce a son.' 'My wife can only have girls.' So the refrains go.

Countless women, at the birth of a girl, have had to endure the commiseration, tacit or overt, of their friends and relations; the resentment and hostility of their husband or in-laws; and the humiliation of feeling themselves accused of being unable to produce male children. They have experienced distress, guilt and a sense of unworthiness at the birth of a girl. They have felt envy for others more 'fortunate' or 'better' than themselves. Some have even been rejected by their husbands for this reason.

In the less privileged sections of the population, where male and female stereotypes are most pronounced and variations least tolerated, such prejudice is even stronger. How many working-class women have been sent on laborious pilgrimages to special shrines by implacable mothers-in-law or angry husbands in order to pray for the desired son?

But even in the more privileged classes where one might expect some knowledge of scientific fact, many people still believe that it is the woman who determines the sex of the child. Others go so far as to say that the woman is responsible for producing females and the man for producing males, as though a battle were being waged between ovum and sperm, the winner having power to give life to an individual of his or her own sex.

A young pregnant philosophy graduate says: 'There were five girls in my family. Let's hope I don't repeat my mother's mistakes. My husband is a bit worried by this precedent in my family because he would like a son.'

The mother-in-law of a respectable middle-class family confides: 'I had four fine healthy boys. Let's hope my daughter-in-law *will do as well*. My son would be delighted if his first child were a boy.'

The supremacy of the male and the inferiority of the female are basic values in a patriarchal culture. It is understandable that in such a culture the man's prestige should never be questioned, since this could undermine his power. In fact, the various beliefs about motherhood – from the most ancient to the most contemporary – have always attributed to the man the merits and the dominant rôle in the process of reproduction, while leaving the mistakes and the secondary rôle to the woman.

Aristotle affirmed that the human embryo developed from a coagulate of the menstrual flow. That is, woman provided the formless matter while man had the more noble rôle of giving it form.

Even this was an enlightened viewpoint, since most of his contemporaries considered that the woman contributed nothing of her own to the baby's conception and only nourished the seed provided by man. Aeschylus in the *Eumenides* wrote: 'The mother of him who is called her child is not the creator, but merely the nurse of the young life which is sown in her.'

In the very early days of embryology, opinions were divided between those who believed in the predominance of the paternal rôle and those who were convinced of the dominance of the maternal rôle. Little by little, it was established that man and woman contributed equally to the process of reproduction: twenty-three chromosomes in the ovum and twenty-three in the sperm. But it was only in 1956 that the existence of spermatozoa carrying X chromosomes and spermatozoa carrying Y chromosomes was discovered.

With the degree of present knowledge, how is it still possible that educated women can ask their husband's forgiveness for having given birth to a daughter?

Prejudices are deeply rooted in tradition. They defy time, correction and contradiction because they are socially useful. Human insecurity needs certainties, and prejudices supply these. Their stupefying strength resides precisely in the fact that they are not transmitted to adults who – as conditioned as they may be – may still have enough of even an impoverished critical sense to analyse and refute them. Prejudices are passed on as indisputable truths in childhood and are never again questioned.

In spite of himself, the individual absorbs such prejudices. The one who formulates them and defends them is as much their victim as the one who suffers and is marked by them. To refute and destroy such prejudices requires not only great strength of mind, but also the courage of rebellion, which not everyone has. Rebellion arouses hostility, and those who attempt to undermine the unwritten laws of convention, deeper and more tenacious than any written laws, may be socially condemned and indeed, ostracised. And where can women find the courage to oppose such prejudices when by the very education which is reserved for them, they are programmed to lack courage? Their sense of inferiority and insecurity, their conviction that they ought to pay any price in exchange for consideration and security, makes them into conservatives who fear change – even if this change were to be to their advantage in the long run.

Let us examine the prejudice which holds men's bodies to be perfect where procreation is concerned. This becomes particularly evident when a couple is apparently sterile. All clinical tests are then first carried out on the woman, and only when these have produced no result – and not always even then – does the reluctant and humiliated male consent to undergo tests in his turn. This is all the more extraordinary when one considers that the male genitalia are much more easily accessible than the female, and an examination of them or a test for sperm fertility is infinitely simpler, less painful and less expensive than say, an examination of the uterine tubes.

When a woman gives birth to an abnormal baby, she always feels guilty and seeks precedents in her own family which may confirm her responsibility. The man, on the other hand, will deny responsibility, shift it on to his partner and never think of doubting his own perfection. The man, in other words, seems to require incontrovertible proof – which he takes care not to solicit – before he will believe himself inadequate, while the woman always believes herself to be guilty until the opposite is proved.

When it comes to accepting prejudices directed against them, women's passivity is boundless. Precisely the most numerous and deeply rooted prejudices concern women's relations with men, with family and children. Although reality proves the contrary to be true, women are all inwardly persuaded that children guarantee the stability of a marriage, keep a couple together, help it to overcome difficult moments or even prevent them. When a marriage does in fact enter a crisis period, women will often resort to having a baby – an extreme measure, but according to them an infallible one. They are convinced that this can give new life to the marriage. Many of them believe that a childless marriage is doomed to failure, and similarly that motherhood is the only real fulfilment possible for a woman. And while the world is glutted with unhappy, frustrated mothers, they stubbornly insist on seeing themselves as diminished in their femininity if they do not succeed in becoming mothers – and mothers of males.

Boy or girl?

The waiting period is dominated by this question which cannot be answered, at least not here. In the United States, however, it is possible to undergo a special test after the fifth month of pregnancy to discover whether the baby will be a boy or a girl.[1] Many popular customs exist aimed at guessing the sex of a baby. If these are examined closely they all betray the desire to have a male child. Some even preempt the question by going straight to the heart of the matter and suggesting ways of conceiving a male. For example, having intercourse when there is a crescent moon or when the moon is full (it is inadvisable to have intercourse when there is a new moon as one might have a deformed child), lying on one's right side and so on. Other time-tested recipes are invoked only when conception has already taken place in order to satisfy the legitimate curiosity of the parents to be.

In some regions, the seeds in a handful of grain are counted: if the number is uneven it will be a boy, if even, a girl.

If a coin slipped down the back of the mother's dress falls on the ground head up, she will give birth to a boy, otherwise it will be a girl.

One of the most common is the wishbone test. The man and woman each take hold of one end of a wishbone and pull it apart.

If the longest part comes away in the man's hand, the baby will be a boy.

If you suddenly ask a pregnant woman what she has in her hand and she looks at her right hand first, she will have a boy; if she looks at her left hand it will be a girl.

A jutting out stomach during pregnancy means that the baby is a boy (clearly an allusion to the penis), while a large, flat, spreading stomach indicates that the baby is a girl.

If the mother's belly is bigger on the right-hand side a boy will be born, and also if her right breast is bigger than her left, or if her right foot is more restless.

If a woman is placid during pregnancy she will have a boy, but if she is bad-tempered or cries a lot, she will have a girl.

If her complexion is rosy, she is going to have a son; if she is pale, a daughter.

If her looks improve, she is expecting a boy; if they worsen, a girl.

In the same way, a difficult pregnancy with swollen legs, a feeling of weight on the pelvis and marks on the skin is said to indicate a girl.

If the foetal heartbeat is fast, it is a boy; if it is slow, it is a girl.

If the foetus has started to move by the fortieth day it will be a boy and the birth will be easy, but if it doesn't move until the ninetieth day it will be a girl. This is related to another earlier belief. Before the theologians came to the conclusion that the soul entered the foetus at the moment of conception, they had a theory that for males this happened eighty-nine days after conception, while for females it happened thirty-nine days later. This was of course only after they had ascertained that women had souls at all – a doubt which had a long history.

If we examine the examples above, we can see that they have a common characteristic. Those factors which announce the birth of a boy are always the positive ones. In effect, an odd number implies a 'something more' as opposed to the even number. In the wishbone test, the long part carries the general significance of the male's superior worth, but also transparently alludes to that anatomical 'something more' that the male possesses. Good humour, rosy colouring, early movement of the foetus, the crescent moon, the coin that falls head up, the jutting out stomach, all these are 'positive' indications. Furthermore, many of the presages of the male sex refer to the right-hand side of the body which is considered to be the more important, more noble, stronger and more active side. The right hand is used for greeting, making pacts, summoning, refusing, writing, blessing, eating, working and using a weapon. The important guest sits at the right hand of his host, Etiquette demands that the right-hand side of the pavement be yielded to a person to whom one owes respect. On the other hand, to place the left foot on the ground first when getting out of bed is seen as an evil omen. The adjective 'sinister' derives from the Latin for left and left-handedness is still regarded as odd; even today there are people who try to correct it.

Some of these popular beliefs, because they are linked to a peasant culture, have completely disappeared. But many are still very much alive, not only among the lower classes.

A young pregnant woman told me that in her office (she works for the management of a big firm) her colleagues of both sexes, all of whom were graduates, had not only given her an elaborate set of instructions for preventing the child's being born with a birthmark, but had also suggested a strange way of foretelling the sex of the child. She should ascertain whether her right buttock was larger than the left one, in which case she would certainly have a boy.

All these factors already indicate the sexual stereotypes present in our culture and they reveal how deeply these models must be rooted in us if we tend to attribute to children characteristics considered to be typical of one or the other sex even *before they are born*.

Since it is actively *desired* that boys should be more lively and forceful than girls – who are *expected* to be calm and passive – the movements of the foetus are interpreted in this light. It is true that a continuity and correlation do exist between the activeness of the foetus and that of the newborn child: this activity is a manifestation of its constitutional temperament. But it is equally true that a male foetus can become a very inactive little boy, while there are little girls who are very energetic and lively. Not to take both points of view into consideration can only lead to wholly arbitrary generalisations.

The game of expecting different characteristics from the sexes begins here, before the baby is even born, and will go on for ever. From time immemorial, boys have been conditioned to be active and aggressive and girls to be passive and submissive. It is then assumed that this behaviour stems naturally from the biological make-up of the sexes. The exceptions which appear, however numerous, are regarded only as exceptions and the prejudices remain.

Hostility towards the female sex

When we attribute to others personal and often negative feelings, we are in fact making a projection. This is an unconscious defence mechanism against impulses that have been rejected as unacceptable by the ego; and even well-balanced personalities are not free of these impulses. An instance of this attribution to another of one's own hostile impulses lies in the widespread belief that a boy is born with greater ease than a girl, as though the foetus participated in some way in the process of giving birth, and the boy, being stronger, livelier and more active than the girl would make some effort to come into the world. The truth is that a girl is less wanted than a boy, and often not wanted at all, her social value being lower than that of the male. But these negative feelings cannot be voiced because they conflict with another tenacious prejudice, namely that one *must* love children. Not to love a child is a very serious offence. And so the situation is reversed and hostility *towards* the female child is interpreted as the hostility *of* the female child in the womb towards her mother. It can be so strong as to complicate the actual act of giving birth – a physiological act in which the foetus is totally passive.

> Bad labour pains are attributed to the girl. The girl *by her very nature* is a source of pain from the start. Even during the first months and years of life girls are still thought to be more whining and troublesome than boys.[2]

The widespread belief that girls cry more than boys is another example of unconscious hostility towards the female. Anyone who is used to newborn babies will know that the opposite is true, although it cannot be categorically affirmed. It is certainly true that there are babies who cry desperately as soon as they are born and continue to do so for many days, and those who cry very little and sleep a lot. The sex of the baby seems to have nothing to do with it.

The way the birth unfolds does influence the newborn baby, but so does the cold, the violent lighting in the delivery room, the unpleasantly cold contact of the rubber gloves which hold him, the lack of gentleness with which he is handled, washed and dressed, the temperature of the water in which he is bathed, the suddenness with which he is immersed and the infinite number of brutal manipulations to which he is subjected in the moments following birth. But the reactions of newborn babies to environmental stimuli depend on innate temperamental differences. The degree of sensitivity to environmental stimuli is different for each baby and probably depends on the child's physical make-up: how sensitive it is to temperature, how tolerant of noise, light, being handled or moved and how great its need is for physical contact with another human being. Reactions also manifest themselves in different ways. The baby who does not appear to react to brusque, hurried treatment may be suffering in a passive, internal way containing his distress and taking refuge in compensatory behaviour such as prolonged sleep or thumb-sucking. Another will more openly manifest agitation by cries and anxious behaviour.

Boys are preferred

It is difficult to describe how much peasants suffer if they have too many daughters. Their reasons certainly sound plausible. They know that when the time comes for marriage the girl will impoverish the household, not only by giving up her domestic duties but by taking her dowry with her. At the same time, they see that girls do not have enough physical strength for labour in the fields. Thus when a girl is born, the men of the family sigh, fearing to see their agricultural tools lying idle from lack of hands. But because they like to predict according to their desires, they have taken up the following custom. An uneven number of eggs is brought to the house of a mother who has just given birth to a daughter. They believe that by doing this they are assuring the birth of a son next time, even though this remedy has often been seen to fail.[3]

Times have changed. Peasants and their families are disappearing from the countryside and becoming urbanised. Their daughters go out to work quite young, indeed before the sons who study longer. Daughters bring money home instead of taking it out in the way described in the above extract. Therefore they contribute to their respective families as much and possibly more than sons, who often spend more. The women work, at least before marriage. The problem of economic dependence on the family is removed,

so that one would expect the birth of a girl to be greeted with
cries of joy. The daughter is a productive being, able to work and
to bring home money, not to mention to take over the domestic
work which will be forced on her as soon as possible, so thoroughly
that she will never escape from it again. She is a being equipped
with formidable energy and enviable strength since she can accomplish what no boy would ever have the energy to do: a real triple
feat, made up of housework, a job, and the procreation and upbringing of children.

But nobody rejoices. It is still the boy who is awaited, preferred,
longed for.

The fact is, that although the structure of society may be changing more and more rapidly, man's psychological structure changes
very slowly. For thousands of years man has held the power, and
he cannot bear the thought that this will cease with his death. He
wants to pass it on to a being like himself. Whoever holds power
has immense prestige: he takes on the proportions of a symbol; he
has the right and the duty to realise his potential to the full; he
is expected to be an individual, and he is valued for what he
will be.

The female is expected to become an object, and she is valued
for what she will *give*. Two completely different rôles. The man's
rôle allows him to make full use of his talents and powers and
encourages his egoism, while the woman must renounce personal
aspiration and suppress her own will so as to allow others to
achieve theirs. The world runs on this suppressed female energy,
which is there like a great reservoir at the disposal of those whose
own energy is employed in the pursuit of power.

The birth of a son, particularly if he is the first child, is for a
man an apotheosis, a triumph. If conceiving a child gives the male
a comforting proof of his virility, the birth of a son provides him
with the complete, perfect, insuperable expression of his own
potency. Virility creating virility, perfection made flesh.

The most common ambition nowadays is to have only two
children, first a boy and then a girl. If the first is a girl, then the
second must be a boy. If the first is a boy, then a second boy will
also be welcomed. But if two daughters are born, the second is
always a disappointment. At this point the planning gets out of
hand, the number of children planned rises to three, and waiting
for the son becomes fraught with anxiety. If he arrives, the game
is over; but if not the problem becomes more complex and panic

sets in. The conflict between the decision to have no more children and the desire to have the longed-for son becomes fierce. How many women owe their birth to their parents' attempt to have the desired son?

This frantic desire to have children of different sexes but with a clear preference for boys would not exist if the expectations of the parents were not so radically different for each sex. In fact, if each child were regarded as a unique individual with his own potential, and were offered as much help as possible to develop in his own way, the question of sex would automatically lose its importance. Instead, the boy is desired for his maleness, for the prestige that his birth brings to the family, for the authority he will have in the family and outside it, and for what he will achieve. The girl is only wanted – if she is wanted at all – on the basis of a sort of scale of convenience.

Girls are:

– more affectionate (the parents expect to be loved more by girls than by boys, who are not at all affectionate)

– more grateful (the horrific nature of the blackmail reveals itself; such a degree of gratitude is never expected of boys)

– sweet and playful (they are objects, mere playthings)

– more fun to dress (they are not worth anything in themselves but in their appearance; it is not their intelligence but their beauty which counts)

– company in the home (nobody expects a boy to be company; as soon as he can he goes out)

– a help with the housework (not only are boys not expected to do housework, they are prevented from doing it since they are destined for greater things).

And yet, in spite of these opinions on their affectionate nature, sweetness, their submissiveness and capacity for work, and in spite of the fact that their upbringing tends to cost less because they usually receive less education than boys, it is commonly held that it is harder to bring up girls. Why?

It is much more difficult and tiring to suppress and erode what are often powerful energies, than it is to give free flow to such drives and stimulate them towards achieving something concrete. It is easier to encourage someone to develop in his own way than to repress the driving forces which are present in every person regardless of sex.

The girl whose development has been inhibited is obliged to resort to some sort of self-defence mechanism if she is not to succumb, especially in cases where her drives were particularly strong and a great deal of intervention was needed to repress them. Such a girl exhibits character traits which are not, as people think, typical of the female sex but which are simply produced by the psychological castration which she has been forced to undergo. Little girls who seem discontented, spoilt, whining, lazy, self-destructive, bored, inert, apathetic or rebellious against everything and everyone without reason, and unsure of what results they want to achieve by this behaviour are the products of this psychological castration. They are impotent beings who are acutely conscious of their condition and fight against it fearfully, uncertainly, timidly. They are locked in a state of perpetual ambivalence towards themselves and others.

In spite of the marked general preference for males, where adoption is concerned girls are preferred. At first, this phenomenon appears as a victory for the female sex. However, as soon as an assessment is made of the reasons for which a childless couple decide to adopt a girl, the matter appears in a different light. In adoption, practical considerations are of determining importance: the beauty and grace of little girls, the satisfaction of looking after their appearance; the company they will provide for their parents, especially for the mother (husbands often consent to adoption for the wife's sake); the adoptive mother's feeling of 'not knowing how to treat a boy – with a girl I would feel more at ease'; the assumption that a daughter will stay closer to one than a boy because boys are 'more independent' while a girl stays close to the family even after she marries; and the fact that it is not necessary to find her a profession since she will find a husband to keep her.[4] Besides this, in the case of adopted children the spectre of heredity always rears its head. As it is the male who assumes and passes on the family name, any bad behaviour on his part caused by hereditary factors will have greater social repercussions than if he were a female.

In Lucania, when a boy is born, a pitcher of water is poured into the road to symbolise that the newborn baby's destiny is to travel the roads of the world. When a girl is born, water is thrown on to the hearth to show that she will lead her life within the walls of the home. Elsewhere, such symbolic gestures are not made. But the reality remains the same.

Systematic conditioning is required to produce individuals who consent to a rôle for which they have been destined since before their birth.

The first element of differentiation appears symbolically in the colour of the layette prepared for the baby. Because the baby's sex is unknown, a layette is bought in colours which are suitable for a boy or a girl, pink being rigorously excluded even by those who wish for a daughter. Pink is thought of as a particularly feminine colour, unthinkable for a boy. The people who sell baby clothes are obviously well aware of this as they sell pink clothes only for babies already born. This phenomenon is all the more surprising when one realises that the use of pink and blue to distinguish the two sexes is comparatively recent. The fashion for coloured ribbons to announce the birth of a baby was apparently initiated by a Bolognese midwife as late as 1929 and the custom has since extended to various accessories including the cards which families send out to announce a birth.[5]

How could such a recent development take such deep root, unless it were related to the much more long-standing convention which calls for maximum differentiation of the sexes? Why does the idea of a newborn boy dressed in pink arouse reactions of real repulsion when his face can rarely be distinguished from that of a girl? Even in decorating the baby's room, the adult only feels at ease if he has done his best to create a décor which he considers suited to the sex of the baby. This again shows him to be aware that he must intervene very early on in order to obtain the required behavioural pattern of his child. A boy's room is usually decorated in a more practical, less frivolous way than a girl's. Blue and bright colours predominate; there is no flowered wallpaper or excessive ornamentation. A baby girl's room is much prettier. It is full of frills and flounces, and pastel tones abound even if there is no actual pink. And so, even before the appearance in a boy of any such recognisably 'masculine behaviour' as aggression, voracity, liveliness, restlessness, robust crying, the signpost of a pre-established colour is provided, a readily comprehensible symbol that will immediately declare the child to be a male.

All this reveals that people are much more conscious than one might think that sex is not determined once and for all by anatomical features, but that a child has to acquire his sexual identity through the culture of his own social group; and that the surest way for the child to acquire this is to assign him sexual attitudes and models of behaviour which do not allow any ambiguity. And this is done from the very start. The more these models differ for boys and girls, the greater the guarantee of a successful result. This is why from earliest infancy, everything that could make the two sexes similar is eliminated and whatever can make them different is emphasised.

He is born

'It's a boy!' 'It's a girl!' These are the first words spoken by the obstetrician when a baby is born, in reply to the mother's mute or explicit question. The baby is quite ignorant of the question of which sex he belongs to, and will be so for a long time. But some-one will preoccupy herself with the matter for the time being, someone who already has clear notions of the ideal models of masculinity or femininity. The son or daughter must conform to these models as closely as possible, whatever the cost. If the parents' expectations of their children are determined to such a degree by the child's sex, they will inevitably react accordingly from the very first moment they hold the child in their arms. This simple fact ensures that children of different sexes have completely different experiences of life.

In theory, the father's rôle in bringing up children is secondary. In fact, he does maintain control of the mother's treatment of the child. He further acts as a model for the son to imitate and identify with, while for a daughter he provides a masculine image. But it is the mother who finally shapes both male and female. She will model the girl after herself in accordance with the image approved by men. She will model the boy in the image to which she has had plenty of time to adapt during childhood, adolescence and youth. It is not difficult. All she has to do is to re-enact with him the same tolerant, compliant accomplice's attitude, which she main-tains towards adult men.

What happens between a mother and her newborn son? What happens between a mother and her newborn daughter? There can be no doubt that the mother anticipates a certain type of response or reaction from her baby depending on its sex. But what can she do to make the child modify behaviour of which she does not approve because this does not conform to the expected pattern?

The newborn baby does not know who he is or where he is. He knows nothing about his body, his surroundings or his mother. He is virtually immobile and the satisfaction of his many needs depends entirely on the person who cares for him. She knows of him only what she wishes to interpret. Some of his needs are particularly urgent and acute, and produce unbearable stress if they are not satisfied. This is the terrain on which he meets his mother and it is precisely the way in which she deals with his demands which will shape his habits and his experience and his conditioning. Allport says:

> How the baby is carried, whether he is securely wrapped, whether he is fed on schedule or on demand, at what stage he is weaned, how he is punished, if he is, what happens if he is in a bad temper when he is bathing or when he dirties himself, how he is washed, what happens when he touches sexual organs: these are all significant questions for those who maintain that the child's fundamental personality is formed in the first years of life.[6]

Feeding is certainly the most important event in the day of a newborn baby, since it satisfies its strongest need to be nourished. This activity is full of emotional implications, and it is repeated as many as five to seven times a day. Lézine states that in a sample of babies of both sexes that was studied,[7] 34% of the mothers refused to breast-feed their daughters either because they regarded it as forced labour, or because they were prevented by their work which took first priority.

But with one exception, all the mothers of boys wanted to breast-feed. Could one advance the hypothesis that out of the remaining 66% of the sample who breast-fed their daughters a percentage did it unwillingly? Certainly, one could apply the same hypothesis to some of those 99% of mothers who breast-fed their sons, but this almost unanimous adherence leads one to suppose that a mother has less difficulty in deciding whether to breast-feed a boy. It is possible that another factor contributes to this decision: the widespread conviction, which is in fact correct, that boys are more delicate than girls (106 boys are born for every 100 girls but the infant mortality rate is much higher for boys) and so they have a greater need of their mother's milk. But there may also be the desire to see them grow as big and strong as possible, that is, real boys in every way. Also women are conditioned, and few can escape it, to think that it is the duty of a woman, whether she be daughter, wife or mother, to put herself in the service of the male and not neglect the least of his needs. Girls, on the other hand, are used to sacrificing themselves from a very early age.

Otherwise, 'what would they do when they grow up?' Thus, if they are not given the best from the start, it is 'for their own good'.

The peculiarly intimate relationship that can exist between a mother and son rarely exists between a mother and daughter. Breast-feeding gives a certain amount of erotic pleasure, caused by the baby stimulating the nipples. It seems more acceptable, more 'natural' if this stimulation is given by a male rather than a female, even though many women would deny the existence of this pleasure. They say that boys are greedier than girls (that is, they are expected to be) and it is well known that the production of milk is directly related to the child's demands: the more the breasts are emptied, the more milk they produce. This could be one of the reasons for boys being breastfed for a longer period but it certainly does not provide a reason for the mother to undertake breast-feeding in the first place.

Girls are usually weaned earlier than boys. Since mothers do not appear to get much pleasure out of feeding them or to consider it so necessary for their growth, it is understandable that they should find it easier to stop feeding girls. Lézine observes that in the group they studied:

> all the girls were completely weaned at three months and had begun mixed feeding at one and a half months, while 30% of the boys were breastfed beyond the fourth month, and 20% continued mixed feeding until the the eighth month. The girls stopped the bottle at twelve months on average, the boys at fifteen months. Boys spent a longer time on the actual feed; at two months boys were spending forty-five minutes at the breast while girls got twenty-five minutes; for bottle-fed babies the time (at six months) was eight minutes for girls and fifteen minutes for boys.[8]

Being breast-fed, and for a sufficiently long time, is an advantage from the psychological as well as the physical point of view. The baby obtains tangible proof of the availability to him of his mother's body and thus of the importance of his own body. The physical intimacy between mother and son that arises from the child's enjoyment of his mother's breast reassures him both of the importance of his well-being to his mother and of the place he occupies in his mother's life and therefore in the world. This guarantee is a profound one which extends through the length of his days, as feed follows upon feed. The signs of affection which accompany the feed give the child the intimate conviction that his

L.G.—2

body is worthy of love, that it is beautiful. The immediate response of his mother, communicated through physical contact, teaches him that his body is something warm and good, and beautiful in itself. It is precisely this complete acceptance of the baby's body by his mother that engenders that self-love which is so rare in girls and often so excessive in boys.

In the above facts concerning the different weaning times for boys and girls and the different lengths of their feeds, it is difficult not to perceive the result of the mothers' pressing demand. In cases of early weaning the mothers I questioned tended to give justifications of a practical nature: return to work, other children to look after, domestic commitments, tiredness, or a delicate state of health often described as 'exhaustion'. But it is symptomatic that such justifications were more common in the case of girls. It would seem that since boys eat more, are fed for longer and take a longer time over each feed, they really should wear out their mothers even more.

I have heard of two boy babies who were breast-fed for an exceptionally long time: one till he was a year and a half old, the other until he was two and a half. Of course, they were not fed only from the breast. They ate normally on the whole, but continued to have two breast-feeds a day, the first an evening and night feed, the second an evening and morning feed. The mothers in question had both decided to wait and see how long their sons really wanted to feed, and to 'let nature take its course'. The first baby gave up both feeds at once, the second gave up the morning feed first and only at two and a half did he give up the evening one. Is it only a coincidence that both these babies were boys? In the case of the baby who was breast-fed till two and a half the mother already had a little girl, who, according to her had spontaneously stopped sucking towards the age of eight months. In the other case the baby was an only child and the mother was not therefore in a position to make comparisons. But to the question of whether she would have breast-fed a girl equally long, she thought for a while before answering that she would certainly do it, but that she was sure that a girl 'would never want to be fed for so long' because 'girls become independent sooner than boys, who are greedy creatures'.

Or would it be more exact to say that it is the mothers who took less pleasure in feeding girls? In any case, the two mothers agreed in asserting that their sons, who are now five and six years old, are extremely active, creative, independent, sociable, always happy, and full of love of life and people.

Where the average length of individual feeds is concerned, there are many things to be taken into account. The fact that boys are considered to be greedier than girls, but at the same time take a longer time to finish their feeds is apparently contradictory. In fact, a very hungry baby should feed more quickly. The reason for the difference found between the time that a boy takes to feed and the time that a girl takes is attributable to the more or less frequent and prolonged pauses conceded to the sucking baby by its mother. It has been observed that a baby sucks three to four times for each swallow. Sucking is an act which uses not only the muscles of the face and mouth, but requires the sucking baby to exert his whole body, using up a great deal of energy. This means that sucking is very tiring for him and forces him to pause frequently to take his breath and to rest. Tolerance to these pauses, which vary from one baby to another, shows the extent of a mother's willingness to participate emotionally and physically in the act of feeding. The process of sucking and swallowing is perfectly understandable to an adult. He does it himself. And its function is clear: suck and swallow. But the pause seems to be a complete waste of time, deliberate laziness on the part of the baby ('he's a lazy feeder', mothers often say), unless the mother can view the creature she is feeding in a less authoritarian way. If she can allow him the freedom to rest, *not to act* during a process of which action is the essential part, this means that she can successfully put herself 'in his shoes', intimately understand him. She regards him as an individual worthy of respect, who expresses his unique personality through his own special rhythm and his own particular needs. It is difficult enough to have tolerance and respect for an equal, let alone a helpless little creature whose excessive dependence is often irritating.

It is these first apparently insignificant concessions to the baby's individuality that demonstrate the mother's sympathy or hostility. And if she is basically hostile, she will feel the need to deny him freedom, to bend him to her will, to impose a discipline on him and to tame him as early as possible, and for ever. The need to impose herself from the start and tame the child seems to be felt more strongly when the child is a girl. A boy, however small and helpless, is already the symbol of an authority to which the mother must submit, and she is often quite happy to do so. The two engage in a reciprocal tyranny, a kind of amorous game, but rarely reach open conflict.

Where little girls are concerned, on the other hand, the greater speed of feeds can be attributed to repeated pressure from the mother. Using all possible means, the mother communicates to her daughter: 'Hurry up.' It is not difficult to induce little babies to hurry their feeds. One need only see what goes on in children's homes and day-nurseries, where because staff are chronically scarce and completely unprepared psychologically, they try to stimulate the child into speeding up the feed by jogging him when the sucking rhythm slows down, by pinching his cheeks or trying to remove the teat from his mouth whenever he pauses for too long, and even by holding him in an uncomfortable position so that he senses that it is no good trying to rest. In fact babies and older children in children's homes take much less time over their meals than children brought up in families. This training is imposed on them in the first weeks of life and quite soon the stimulus is no longer necessary, the baby having become very quick.

A mother communicates her mood and her wishes perfectly to the baby she is feeding. The acute sensitivity of a newborn baby to the way he is held is well-known. From the tenseness of his mother's muscles, from the way she carries out the preliminaries of the feed, from the speed or slowness of her movements which reveal the degree of her haste, and, at a deeper level, communicate her hostility or affection, he very soon learns whether he is going to be allowed to abandon himself peacefully to the pleasures of the feed, or whether these are going to be denied him. There is a way of saying: 'Get on with it!' or 'Take your time', that a newborn baby apprehends from the least gesture of the person who is feeding him. He is not yet able to interpret his mother's facial expressions (though he soon will be, to the extent that in the second month he will answer a smile with a smile), nor to understand the words she addresses to him (although he is very receptive to the gentleness or roughness of her voice). But he is in such close and habitual contact with her body that he is made perfectly aware of his mother's attitude by the impatient movement of an arm, a sudden change of position, the way she offers or withdraws her body, the insecurity or comfort in which he is held, or the caresses which are given or withheld. The newborn baby expresses distress quite clearly. The next step is to find out what he wants and to try to provide it, because he cannot bear his distress. The relationship between a mother and child should stem from the mother's ability to adapt herself to the child's needs, but only too often it is the child who has to adapt to the mother.

As we have already said, greed is considered to be characteristic of baby boys. In fact there are simply some newborn babies who are greedy and some who are not. The animal-like physicality of the baby who avidly attacks the breast or teat is regarded as normal in a boy, proof of his 'natural' aggressiveness and sensuality; but a girl is supposed to have a much more moderate appetite, to be more 'spiritual', less attached to earthly pleasures. Thus, while no one ever interrupts a boy during his feed to moderate his greed, the girl who sucks in too greedy a way is interrupted by having the teat taken from her mouth, by being made to wait until she will approach the breast with more 'feminine grace'. Greed and grace do not go together.

I have often heard women who have fed greedy girl babies complain of it as a defect and express the hope that they will change. This preoccupation is sometimes projected on to the girl's future looks: 'she'll grow into a fatty'. A more honest expression of her real feelings was given by the woman who said, 'She's so greedy, it's disgusting.' What is required of a newborn girl is that she should feed quickly, with a regular rhythm, taking only enough to satisfy her and without showing exaggerated pleasure.

I have been present when particularly hungry, active, robust girls a few days old were being 'trained to be delicate'. The method used consisted in offering the breast or bottle to the baby, who would attack it with some force, and then removing the nipple or teat every so often by closing the baby's nostrils, so that to breathe she had to open her mouth and let go. She was made to wait a moment and then was given the breast or bottle again. If the baby was 'violent' again, the mother interrupted her again, at the same time voicing her disapproval calmly or with irritation. This treatment, repeated each time the baby girl failed to do what was required, obtained the desired result in a very short time. The baby actually managed to control her impulses, taking the teat cautiously, as though trying it out, and only subsequently did she begin to alternate energetic sucking with controlled sucking, until her original confidence and vigour had gone and the feeds began to have a calmer and more uniform flow. Of course the baby's adapting to the required behaviour provoked gently spoken words, caresses and hugs from her mother, indicating that this time she had behaved correctly and was approved of. This sort of training repeated continuously, is enough to establish a permanent pattern of behaviour. Though this kind of treatment is also given to boys, it is applied more frequently and vigorously to girls, simply because they are begrudged physical pleasure.

Given that for a long time sucking is the greatest pleasure that a baby is given to experience and to seek, actively and autonomously, and that it is closely related to the pleasant, reassuring sensation of a full stomach and satisfied hunger, one can easily understand how the significance of oral pleasure extends until it is identified with pleasure in general. Many things will later be found to confirm this. It should always be borne in mind that a little baby feels checks on his impulses to be acts of hostility against himself, rather than against the particular impulse. And he is right. When we act in a repressive way towards him it is because we are in reality hostile to him.

Newborn babies suck for nourishment, but they also suck when their stomachs are full, because it is pleasurable. They do not have many opportunities to give themselves pleasure, but they do at least have a thumb to suck; at first, only by chance, but later on, by deliberately seeking it. From the absorption, concentration and dedication with which they suck, it is evident how satisfying they find this habit. The inhibited, authoritarian adult is made uneasy by this innate ability of the baby to seek and find pleasure in his own body, without asking permission (which the adult would not in any case grant), and he intervenes in subconscious anticipation of something which would embarrass him even more – masturbation. In fact he prefers to provide the baby with a substitute, in the form of a dummy, because then the baby has to ask him for it.

In this way, the adult protects his own importance and authority. He can give the dummy or take it away at his own pleasure. But he can exercise little control over the thumb because it is part of the baby's body, and for this reason he views the sucking habit, whether unconsciously or not, as an early form of masturbation – still regarded as an unnatural vice.

Whether it is a question of allowing the crying baby the consolation of the dummy, or of allowing him to suck his own thumb in peace, mothers admit that they are stricter with girls and more indulgent with boys. The reasons they give for this are often rationalisations of deeper feelings. Most common is the excuse that the dummy or thumb deforms the dental arch, something which is considered to be much more serious and prejudicial to a girl's looks than to a boy's. Looked at objectively, crooked teeth are no more attractive in a boy than they are in a girl, but because the girl is judged from early childhood as the sexual object which she will become, her physical beauty is of prime importance and her family will fight for it. This is much less true in the case of a boy.

The fact that girls and their mothers do not have a very good relationship is shown by the feeding problems – and sleep problems – of which the mothers complain. Lézine came across:

> difficulties in feeding with 94% of the girls in the sample observed (slowness, vomiting, contrariness) and only 40% of the boys. With 50% of the girls *these appear within the first month*, and their appetite remains small until they are six years old. With boys, difficulties of this type do not appear until later, in the form of contrariness and a variety of demands made on the mother up until the boy's sixth year.[9]

It is evident that mothers feel that the attempts made by their children to conduct their feeds in the way they want constitute an affront and an act of defiance. In girls the inherent conflict does not manifest itself in open rebellion but rather through psychosomatic reactions such as vomiting, digestive upsets, disturbed sleep, difficulty in chewing and swallowing food – that is, in true passive resistance. All the same, Lézine maintains that girls learn to feed themselves sooner than boys, that is

> between twenty-four and thirty months, while most of the boys in this group continue to be helped until they are four to five years old. At table, the boys are more attached to ritual than the girls, and many of them have very elaborate requirements as to the positioning of the things on the table or of their chairs. Here also the mother's attitude is much more rigid with girls, and it is quite usual to be faced with a scene between mother and daughter which makes the meal a trial for the whole family.
>
> In spite of the difficulties made by the boys, *only one mother in this group complains of them as being excessive.* In all the other cases, apart from the usual naughtiness, they regard meals as occasions of joyful communication. The great tolerance which mothers show in this respect has possibly contributed to the great attachment boys have to the meal situation, and their strong desire to prolong the state of dependence which is related to it.[10]

Mothers tell their daughters something to this effect: 'Everything is fine as long as I have to do as little as possible for you, so hurry up and learn how to fend for yourself' – an injunction which is only an apparent urging towards independence and autonomy. In fact, only one kind of self-sufficiency is required from little girls: that which encourages them not to depend on others for the little practical everyday things. Alternatively, she must be completely dependent where more important choices are involved, such as those concerning her self-realisation. And she must put her psychic energies at the service of other people as soon as possible.

With the boys the mother's underlying message is different: 'You can do whatever you want, it's your right. But since I'm willing to continue serving you, don't detach yourself from me' – an attitude in which the boy recognises his right to make the major decisions, and to use whatever is offered him by others in order to realise his potential.

Here is a typical example of a mother encouraging her daughter towards independence in practical matters, yet denying her the freedom to develop as an individual in herself. This young mother of an eleven-month-old baby girl came for a consultation because she could not get her child to behave as she wished her to. The little girl had been weaned towards the end of the third month because, the mother said, she had not much milk and it was not worth complicating her life with mixed feeding. She had changed over on to the bottle in one day, and the baby had adapted to it quite easily. At four months she was only having two bottle feeds out of four. The other feeds consisted of baby foods given from a spoon, which she accepted without apparent protest. By six months she was able to drink her milk straight from the cup, and at eight months she could eat sitting at a low table instead of in her mother's arms. The child swallowed her food quickly and without pausing, as the mother claimed she had done right from the start. Very early a spoon was placed in her hand so that she could try to feed herself. (Had this been done in response to an express demand, it would have been a positive act, but because it occurred as an external imposition, it was in fact, negative.) The little girl had managed so well that at eleven months, long before normal, she was able to pick up food from the plate with the spoon and put it in her mouth, though letting most of the contents fall off. Her mother was seeking advice to cure just this inability to manoeuvre the spoon in the right way, which she saw as a stubborn opposition to her wishes on the part of the child.

When it was explained to her that it simply was not possible for a child of that age to co-ordinate her movements sufficiently with cereal and carry it to her mouth – an action which requires twisting the wrist in such a way as to keep the spoon both perpendicular to it and perfectly horizontal so that the food does not fall off – because greater neuro-muscular maturation would be necessary, the mother reacted with annoyance. She stated that the child had always been precocious, that she could walk and performed in her pot with great regularity, and that while she realised that most children were not so advanced, hers was in so many other ways that to refuse to learn such a simple thing must be pure obstinacy.

This mother's rigidity had produced a tense, timid, silent child, serious, thin and nervous, whose sleep at night was noticeably disturbed. When her mother held her, she would not allow herself to relax into her arms, but remained rigidly confined in her own solitude, staring round unblinking with two enormous melancholy eyes which only knew hostility.

Mothers' different attitudes towards boys and girls are revealed again in a second important aspect of upbringing: toilet training. Lézine observes that:

> In this also, mothers are more demanding of their daughters than of their sons. The average age at which training begins is five months for girls (from one to eight months) and eight months for boys (from two to fifteen months). Problems with potting (refusals, playing up, stubbornness) appear earlier with girls (fifteen to eighteen months) than with boys (twenty four months to four years) and last for less time, as boys tend to react with strong and prolonged opposition and to require endless accompanying rituals.[11]

Toilet training starts with the baby being held on the pot between feeds as well as during feeds, the length of time depending on how long it takes him to produce something. Of course, if he does produce something it is completely fortuitous and unintentional, because a baby only learns to retain his faeces and to deposit them in the right place at the age of two. This ability is simply due to his having attained the neuro-muscular maturity which enables him to control the sphincter muscle. Everything that is done before the age of two helps to establish the conditioned reflex of defecation into the pot, but if the baby does things in the right receptacle before that age it is simply because he has received the appropriate stimulus at the moment he was sitting on the pot. Since he is often held there for hours, it is inevitable that sooner or later he will deposit something in it. Then of course his mother congratulates him, and herself, as though her achievement were the fruit of her enlightened persistence, and not of the endless time the baby was made to spend on the pot.

The perfectly understandable wish of avoiding the work of dirty nappies means she never thinks it too early to start trying to get a baby to deposit his faeces in the right place. Some mothers start in the very first month, sometimes feeding the baby and holding him on the pot at the same time, so as to get him to defecate during the feed. The baby feels discomfort in this situation, and he cannot please his mother, who is ruining two of his pleasures at once, feeding and defecating. And this does not leave many pleasures he can enjoy. If the mother presses the baby to finish his feed in the shortest possible time and simultaneously to produce something in the potty (a result which is rarely achieved and then only by chance), he may develop a strong anxiety caused by the conflict between his desire to comply and his complete inability to do so. The baby may then experience acute distress. Demands of this kind towards an adult would be regarded as sadistic, but sadism towards children is very common and is usually regarded with indifference.

Mothers are also more tolerant of little boys when they soil their pants (even grown men are thought of as being naturally rather 'dirty') than of little girls. The latter are expected to make as few demands as possible, to be clean, careful, and to look after their appearance and their own bodies. Of course such a degree of self-control is only achieved later on, but the goal is constant from the start. Indeed, its existence is essential for producing the required feminine behaviour. If a boy is dirty and untidy, this seems to be in the natural order of things. If a girl is, she is looked upon as an annoyance, and is attributed with the malicious intention of not wanting to keep herself clean. 'She does it on purpose' the mother will say.

For the sum of his mother's attitudes towards his body – pleasure, repulsion, or *both* in sequence, the baby learns to regard his body as good or bad. And he learns either to love or to hate himself.

The newborn baby's body is attended to many times a day.

When a baby is undressed and left naked while his mother cleans him, there is an intense exchange of affection between them, and the pleasure which the mother takes in her baby's body is communicated to him in a variety of ways. There are many ways of cleaning a baby, of washing, drying, scenting, powdering, and dressing him. Hands may caress or handle him roughly. They may rest on him warmly and firmly or else barely touch him. They may be confident or inhibited, hard or soft, intimate or strange, warm or cold. The more the baby's body pleases his mother, the more affectionate and caressing she will be with him. The freer she is of inhibitions and prejudices, the more enjoyment she will get from his body by stroking, tickling and rubbing it. She will be free to demonstrate her affection.

Boys are more readily left naked than girls, for with the latter it is found necessary to instil in them from the start a so-called 'innate' sense of modesty. Mothers often cover up the body of a baby girl who is being washed if there are strangers present, though this rarely happens with a baby boy. On the contrary, great pleasure is taken in his nudity and there are jokes and admiring comments made about his sexual attributes. 'Just look what a little man he is', 'He's got everything in the right place, hasn't he?' 'What do you think you're going to do with that absurd little thing?' 'Just think what you'll be doing with it when you're a bit bigger!' and so on. These phrases, which we have quoted because we have heard them used by mothers, fathers and other relations in front of a baby boy, are quite inapplicable to a baby girl, not only because of the different shape of her sexual organs, but because it must be forgotten for as long as possible, and preferably forever, that she has any such organs. The less her genitalia are mentioned, pointed out, or touched, the better. This difference in the attention given to the sexual organs of girls and boys is further demonstrated by diminutives and euphemisms given to them. In her book 'Bad Language', Nora Galli de Paratesi [12] gives a long list of euphemisms for naming, or better to avoid naming, the sexual parts of the male. Loosely translated from the Italian, these would be *cece* – chick pea; *pisello* – little pea; *bischerino* – little peg; *bacellino* – little pod; *pistolino* – little pistol; *pipino* – little pipe; *pifferino* – little flute; *dondolino* – dangler. In the corresponding paragraph for females there is not one diminutive cited as being used to refer to little girls. This is no mere oversight, but points to a real verbal lacuna. To de Paratesi's repertory could be added; *pescolino* – little fish; *uccelino* – birdie; while all we can come up with for females are *passerina* – little lark, and *pagnottina* – little mite.

It is true that the male sexual organ is more obvious than the female and its exhibition often arouses hilarity, curiosity or interest, as, for example, when a little boy unexpectedly 'wees' in the face of someone standing in front of him; or if he has a proper erection, which can happen very early on, and can cause amused embarrassment in some, open gaiety in others, and even touching and tickling, often accompanied by kisses on the genital area. If a father did this with his baby daughter he would arouse horror. Nor would a mother ever do it with her daughter. Even if the female sexual organs are less obvious, they do still exist, but they are deliberately ignored. It is true that mothers sometimes react to exhibitions of the genitals of boys in a repressive way, using expressions such as 'Little pig, you dirty creature, don't be rude' and so on, but this simply serves to emphasise the existence of the sexual organs not to deny them as is the case with girls. In other words, the sexuality of the baby boy is openly admired, while the girl's is often passed over in silence as though it did not exist. The later it manifests itself the better. It would be best if it never showed itself at all.

When a boy baby first succeeds in catching hold of his genital organs, having already explored other parts of his body – such as the hands which come into his field of vision by chance, and then the feet which are easy to bring up to his eyes – he is greatly helped by their form. He fumbles and finds a lovely toy to play with. The baby girl does not find anything quite so exciting, but both boys and girls play with their genitals at the same stage of development and get obvious pleasure out of doing so. But while in a boy this activity is regarded with a certain indulgence, it is rigidly suppressed in a girl.

Already present in these diverse attitudes towards a baby's earliest sexual activities is the prejudice that boys are endowed with much stronger sexual instincts than girls, and that therefore any erotic activity in them should be tolerated if not exactly encouraged. A girl who indulges, on the other hand, is deviating from the norm and must be restrained. It is quite possible to grow into a woman without ever living one's own sexuality, but one cannot become a man without living it fully. This is part of the creed created by stereotyping.

Mother–daughter relationships are thus much more proble-matic than mother–son relationships right from the first few months. This shows itself in typical conflicts. Mothers confess to being more anxious, more nervous, more insecure when they are bringing up a son, but in spite of this they find it an easier under-taking. They do not blame any of the troubles met in bringing up a girl on themselves, but rather on the 'difficult nature' of girls. With boys, on the other hand, since sleep and feeding problems are seen to be fewer, only open conflicts appear as such. Indeed the problems and conflicts which mothers have with their daughters seem to be related less to the mother's nervousness than to the rigidity of her methods. Mothers themselves recognise that they are stricter with girls.[13]

I would further add that mothers are even more strict and demanding with daughters who are hypertonic, that is active, curious, independent, noisy, early walkers, in other words when they exhibit characteristics generally thought of as male. A *hypo-tonic* girl, that is one who is calm, passive and undemanding accepts her mother's demands without much difficulty because they correspond to her own need for security and order. Here there should be few reasons for a mother and daughter to enter into conflict. But a little girl who is lively and exuberant (tem-peramental characteristics which emerge in the first days of life) is treated in the same way as a hypotonic child and often reacts dramatically. Since this reaction does not fit the stereotyped image either, the adult again intervenes until the girl shows only an approved, 'feminine' sort of aggression, which is expressed in violence towards herself, long periods of crying and self-pity.

A hypotonic or inactive boy baby is stimulated as much as possible in order to make him become reasonably active and aggressive. Such pressure does involve an attack on the child's character. By forcing him to conform to the male stereotype certain qualities are destroyed while others are stimulated. But the damage done will be much less than that suffered by the over-active girl, who is forced to conform to a model whose poten-tial is far lower than her own.

The hypertonic male, like the hypotonic female, is the closest to the stereotype. His mother sometimes reacts against his vitality, but her opposition is limited to details of behaviour, and not to the whole way in which he is brought up as the case is with the hypertonic girl. A mischievous boy is accepted easily. In fact he is encouraged to be so. But the opposite is true for a mischievous girl. Her aggressiveness and curiosity are a threat and all possible methods are used to make her change her way of behaving. Lézine reports the extremely significant case of an over-active, unruly girl. She had begun to walk before the age of twelve months and had always been advanced in every field, according to the tests she had undergone. Major conflicts with her mother had broken out at about eighteen months because of her bois-terousness, and the mother had decided to take a strong line. This mother, a strict, fussy perfectionist, 'liked to have a rule of order in all things'. After a few months, the little girl was brought to reason, became very reliable, applied herself for long periods to a variety of activities so that at three she could knit, at four she could use an iron, and at five she could make the bed by herself. But she spent her nights grinding her teeth, so she was once more submitted to a battery of psychological tests.

> She is nervous, clenches her fists, withdraws her head between her shoulders (age three). She shows herself to be inhibited, trembles, bites her lips (age four). She has controlled, rigid gestures, remains timid and inhibited (age five). She screws up her mouth, talks very softly and has endless manias of tidiness. She rarely plays with other children and prefers quiet games. At school she seems reserved and turned in on herself. One is struck by the precocity of her obsessional tendencies, of her perpetual need to verify and do things with great thoroughness.

And it goes on:

> This state of premature self-control is further aggravated by the activeness of the child and by her frustrated need for movement. Re-examined at seven, she produces a series of anxiety drawings and appears to have phobic tendencies.[14]

It is clear that this little girl is living in the perpetual anxiety of having to suppress her own impulses so as not to arouse the terrific anger of her mother who started experimenting on her when she was a mere eighteen months old and made her realise once and for all how she wanted her to behave. Her desperate attempts to comply with her mother's demands and contain her natural vitality as much as possible make her turn in on herself. She channels her energy into sedentary activities, but without being wholly able to free herself from an acute state of anxiety. She tries to hold this at bay by constructing reassuring but basically phobic rituals which form an alarming defence mechanism.

This case, by virtue of the firmness and decisiveness with which this little girl was repressed, is certainly uncommon. Although it usually takes on a less violent form – one diluted over a longer period of time, but nonetheless efficient – such repression makes victims of the majority of girls whose innate temperament differs too radically from the imposed female stereotype. It is precisely such girls, full of vitality and curiosity, hungry for experience, eager to conquer the world around them and achieve their own autonomy who are destined to fight real battles with their mothers from a very early age with very little hope of ever emerging the victor.

> As Freud has shown, the only really satisfying relationship is that which links the mother to the son, and everything leads one to suppose that even the most affectionate and maternal mother feels ambivalent towards her daughter.[15]

Notes

1 David Rorvik and Kandrum Shettles, *Your Baby's Sex: Now You Can Choose*, Cassels, London.
2 Giovanni Bronzini, *Vita tradizionale in Basilicata*, ed. Montemurro, Matera, p. 43.
3 Giuseppe Pitrè and S. Salomone Marino, in 'Archivio per lo studio delle tradizioni popolari', January–March 1884, p. 329.
4 Bianca Giudetti Serra, *Felicità nell'adozione*, Ferro, Milan 1968, pp. 77–78.
5 Giuseppe Vidossi, *Saggi e scritti minori di folklore*, ed. Bottega d'erasmo, Turin 1960, p. 282.
6 Gordon W. Allport, *Personality: A Psychological Interpretation*, Constable, London 1949.
7 Odette Brunet and Irène Lézine, *I primi anni del bambino*, Armando, Rome 1966, p. 58.
8 Ibid., p. 58.
9 Ibid., p. 58.
10 Ibid., p. 59.
11 Ibid., p. 79.
12 Nora Galli de' Paratesi, *Le brutte parole. Semantica dell'eufemismo*, Mondadori, Milan 1969.

13 Odette Brunet and Irène Lézine, op. cit., p. 161.
14 Ibid., p. 156.
15 Bela Grumberger, 'Le narcissisme dans la sexualité féminine', *La sexualité féminine* edited by J. Chasseguet Smirgel, Petite Bibliothèque Payot, Paris 1972.

CHAPTER 2

EARLY CHILDHOOD

> 'I've got one and you've got none.'
> *Refrain of a three-and-a-half-year-old boy to his*
> *six-year-old sister.*[1]

Alessia is thirteen months old. She is round and rosy, has two short solid legs, lively and very mobile blue eyes and she is almost hairless. She has attended a day nursery since she was a few months old. Each morning, she arrives happily, snatching off her coat in her eagerness to start. She is overflowing with energy and vitality, always good-humoured, laughing, active, curious and noisy. She learned to walk at ten months and now she goes at a great rate, often stumbling, sometimes with disastrous results. Yet she never complains. She gets up and is off again, ready for new adventures.

Always prepared for mischief, she wanders and explores, threading her way into dangerous situations. With a minimum of support she goes very quickly up and down stairs. She climbs on to railings, low walls, gates, chairs, benches and the legs of anyone who shows an interest in her. She is always extremely busy, concentrating on the present, and as long as she is absorbed in the interest of the moment she is completely unaware of what is happening around her.

She drags things around that are heavier and larger than herself. Even if she turns purple with the effort of doing something by herself, she refuses to let anyone help her. She feeds herself and if anyone tries to come to her aid she lets out a savage scream. Her vocabulary, which is limited, varies between the bossy and the polite, with a great deal of 'it's mine' pronounced in stentorian tones and an abundance of 'thank you's' both appropriate and inappropriate.

She calls all children 'baby' but has no name for any adults except her mother. She is not aggressive with the other children whom she loves and whose company she seeks, especially if they are older than she is. She will watch them playing for a long time without joining in their games, and then only sometimes insinuates herself into a group of older children.

When she sees something that another child is holding and wants it, she exclaims loudly, 'It's mine!' but does not try to take the object from its rightful owner. The older children don't pay her much attention, though they sometimes push her. She falls and then gets up looking surprised, as if she hasn't understood, but she doesn't cry. She is fearless and adventurous, always getting into difficult situations, such as climbing on to a gate and then looking rather worried, obviously wondering how she will get down, but confident that things will work out somehow. Her outstanding characteristic is confidence. As soon as she has got out of one problem situation she falls into another. Her desire to prove herself in undertakings that would dismay much bigger children knows no obstacle. She loves the world with passionate enthusiasm, relishes everything that happens around her, and anything that moves. She plays with sand and water, oblivious of everything and everybody, her little face narrowed with concentration on the things that fascinate her, in a sort of trance from which nothing can wake her, not caring that she is sitting in a wet patch or that she is dirty and covered with sand.

Silent and excited, she explores a big chest full of toys and in trying to get hold of something at the bottom which particularly attracts her she ends up by falling right in it, head first. Furiously waggling her legs in the effort to get out, she neither utters a word nor cries for help as though she feels it to be an incident which only concerns her, and from which she does not intend to be rescued by anybody. She emerges from her struggle with the chest, with a red and angry face. Leaving the treacherous object behind, she looks offended, and has a momentary rest on a chair from which she will jump up as soon as she has got her breath back to look once more for new adventures. A boy passes in front of her with a few biscuits in his hand and she is immediately revived. She springs to her feet and follows him exclaiming from time to time, 'Mine!' but he pays no attention. She plants herself in front of him and repeats her demand yet without making any attempt to get the biscuit. The boy turns his back in order to get it away from her, and as he moves, one biscuit falls to the ground. He does not notice, but Alessia does, and quickly picks it up saying 'thank you' in a very loud voice to nobody in particular. She begins to munch it with great enjoyment. Tired from her endless adventure, she seeks momentary refuge in the arms of an assistant, but she soon wriggles away and sets off in search of more excitement.

Alessia is only thirteen months old. She is pugnacious, energetic and strong-willed. She knows what she wants and she wants it at once. She is obstinate, tenacious, patient, proud and dignified. She has few weaknesses. She claims her independence and if the door of the house were opened for her she would go out and never look back except occasionally to seek refuge from her tiredness in loving arms.

What massive weight of repression will be needed to turn this creature – overflowing with vitality, enthusiasm and love of life – into a little lady who is prepared to remain within the walls of an oppressive home and consecrate her energies to the repetitive misery of domestic routine? Given that this is the aim, how much tenacity, how much force, effort, perseverance and hostility will be needed to reduce such a rich being into the rigid mould of what passes as 'femininity'? Alessia is still very young. She has a tranquil, affectionate mother who lets her rampage round at will and regards her with tolerant amusement. She is at an age where it is acceptable for little girls to be failed boys and for little boys to be gentle doll-like creatures. The age does not last for long.

I'm a boy,
I'm a girl

A child very quickly learns to distinguish between male and female. Towards the end of his first year this ability can be tested. If he is shown pictures of adults of both sexes and is asked 'Where is daddy?' 'Where is mummy?' he will point to the figure of the correct sex. The next step towards recognising himself as a being similar to other beings is to recognise himself as a male or female. This happens at around eighteen months.[2] This does not mean that the child can verbally express the concept 'I am a boy' or 'I am a girl' but he *knows* that there are two sexes, that his father and mother are different, and that he is like his father or mother. I have carried out an experiment with some children about two years old who had good verbal capacity. When I asked the girls 'Are you a boy?' they answered immediately and categorically, 'No'. I had the same reaction from the boys when I asked, 'Are you a girl?'

The boys, however, already manifested a certain arrogance in their reply. This is obviously due to a conviction of male supremacy which has been transmitted to them by their families. A typical case was the reaction of a boy just over two who when fondled by an old lady whom he did not know said with some animosity: 'Don't touch me, I'm a boy!' René Zazzo [3] states that at about the age of three the child becomes conscious of his sex. He affirms that at this age a child can actually say whether he is a boy or a girl. Zazzo carried out a survey of children approximately three and a half years old which shows that 'one of the hundred boys questioned by us would rather be a girl; while 15% of the girls said they would prefer to be a boy'. In other words, at the age of three and a half 15% of the girls had not only experienced that typical feminine conflict from which many of them never escape, but were actually able to express their desire to be boys.

A similar survey on sexual preference carried out on slightly older children would almost certainly give even more indicative results. The number of girls unhappy in their 'girlhood' and envious of the masculine condition would undoubtedly have grown. The recognition of oneself as belonging to the male or female sex therefore comes very early on in life and Alessia is quite near to the time when in her unbridled, so-called 'masculine' activity she will discover that she is Alessia, a girl who is like her mother and different from her father. She will recognise her 'potential analogy' with her own mother.

In spite of the varying pressures – examined in the previous chapter – to which children are subjected during their upbringing, it is still difficult at just over the age of one to categorise males and females according to their behaviour. At this age, the sexes still resemble each other and like and choose to do the same things. Differences between them are not very obvious and one constantly has to ask whether these differences are due to the innate temperament of each individual or to his sex. In fact more marked differences of behaviour are often shown between children of the same sex than between children of different sexes. This is all the more true of course for even younger children. Charles Bried [4] states that:

> It is often the case that differences between individuals of the same sex are more outstanding than differences between individuals of different sexes. Therefore when we observe some difference in the behaviour of a boy or girl we cannot decide with any certainty whether this should be attributed to sex or temperament.

Mark is also thirteen months old. He cannot walk yet, though he can stand with only a minimum of support, and can move at a great speed if he is offered a finger to hold. He sits on a rug or at the table and handles various objects for a long time, often putting them in his mouth. If he notices an object some distance away, he will look at it longingly for some time. Only after he has contemplated it sufficiently will he decide to crawl towards it and get it for himself. He is more interested in people than in things. He often asks to be picked up and does so in a most gentle way, holding his head to one side and looking up at the person he wants to charm imploringly, and responding to a smile with an authentically seductive one of his own. He is always seeking physical contact, caresses and tenderness. He does not cry often, but when he does he needs to be consoled for a long time. He listens to words of consolation and accepts comforting caresses with real rapture, uttering happy little sighs. If he is attacked by another child, he does not defend himself, but blinks his eyes in alarm and tries to ward off his aggressor by stretching his arms out in front of himself.

He eats a lot, and with excellent appetite. He likes any food that is offered to him and is very independent about eating solids, which he puts straight into his mouth with his hands. He needs to be encouraged to do things as he is rather slow and contemplative. He much prefers to watch what others are doing than to do anything himself. He sleeps well, and a great deal. His mother treats him as though he were a toy to play with, not paying much attention to what he wants, but he does not protest. If by chance he is involved in an alarming situation, such as getting stuck under his bed, he immediately gives up the struggle and asks for help. If nobody comes to the rescue he doesn't cry or protest; he merely waits anxiously. Once help has come, he shows his gratitude by wanting to be picked up and not put down again. His mother, although she does what she likes with him – for example, putting him to sleep more than necessary – accuses him of being a lie-a-bed and uses every possible method to get him to walk, play, and above all defend himself when attacked by other children. She complains because he does not react against the attacks of his companions. 'What kind of a boy are you?' she often says and then she draws him passionately to her breast saying 'You're mummy's little man.' She dresses him up like a man, wants him to wee standing up like a man, and is proud of his genitals which she considers to be well-developed, and recounts with great pride and in great detail all

the brave deeds that Mark has accomplished. She has great plans
for his future, and can't wait for him to grow up. She already sees
him as someone to lean on.

Since he is a gentle submissive boy, Mark is encouraged to
become more aggressive and more competitive. If he were a girl
he would be left in peace because his behaviour would conform to
type. And his relationship with his mother would probably be less
gratifying for both of them.

The way the child's body moves, the way he copies others, cries
or laughs, is practically identical in both sexes at the age of a year
or a little over, but after this, differences begin to occur. At this
age, the greater aggression attributed to males is not yet evident.
Boys and girls can both be aggressive; but later on the boys'
aggression will continue to be directed towards others while the
girls' is often directed towards themselves. For example, flirtatiousness at one year and even beyond is common to both sexes. Eibl-
Eibesfeldt [5] describes it as an innate behaviour pattern of approach
and flight which has become a ritual inviting pursuit. The author
illustrates this by reproducing a series of photos of a girl of three
who winks and smiles while hiding her face with her hand. It is very
common to see a small boy engaging in the same type of behaviour
in his mother's arms. Addressed by someone he is attracted to, but
does not know very well, he will hide his face in his mother's shoul-
der or behind his hands and smile while winking invitingly. He
catches the eye of the other person with this alternation of provocative mimicry and ritual movements of flight. In fact, he is exhibiting
genuine flirtatiousness. As boys grow older, this kind of behaviour
gradually disappears. In girls it persists precisely because of the
reactions it receives from adults. The girl's flirtatiousness is soli-
cited and encouraged, since she is seen as being already so
'feminine'. In the case of the boy, his attempts at flirtatiousness are
not accepted, and he is taught other patterns of behaviour. It is
because adults do not give any positive response to this type of
seductiveness and at the same time offer more dry, 'masculine'
gestures for the boy to copy that the more effeminate mannerisms
gradually disappear in the boy. Girls, on the other hand, continue
to use them because they copy them from their mothers and from
other women and are encouraged to adopt them by the positive
response that they obtain from adults. It is to be noted that girls
whose mothers are strict and not given to so-called feminine
mannerisms, have a limited and often non-existent repertoire of

flirtatious tricks because they have not had much to imitate. The adult's compliance and condescension teach the girl that she gets far more by acting in this way than by stamping her feet in a rage, or by asking for what she wants in a straightforward, dignified way. Thus she learns to say 'I can't do it', 'I don't know how to', 'help me', in such a charming way as to be irresistible. If her acting the part of a weak, incapable creature who is charmingly imploring gives pleasure to the adult, she will do so because she is anxious to live up to expectation and at the same time get what she wants. This is a mechanism which is learned at the earliest age and functions unfailingly. A woman will use it all her life, paying for it with a loss of autonomy and a sense of frustration which such a loss inevitably generates.

Sexual conditioning can only work in one sex on the understanding that the direct opposite will be produced in the other sex. The superiority of one sex is based exclusively on the inferiority and weakness of the other. If the little boy feels himself to be a little man simply on the basis of domination, someone will have to agree to being dominated. But if boys are no longer taught to dominate and girls no longer taught to accept and love domination, unexpected and hitherto unsuspected expressions of individuality may flourish, far richer, more articulate and imaginative than the restricting, humiliating stereotypes.

Imitation and identification

Conflicts between children and their parents increase noticeably after the first year. Before this, the child's very limited capabilities make him relatively easy to control. He is more submissive than he is later since he is aware of his impotence and dependence on the adult, and also because he is not yet sufficiently motivated by his natural tendency towards autonomy to oppose the will of the adult. Learning to walk, with the resulting increase in independence, partly pleases and partly irritates the adult. The baby, as he gradually achieves the independence – which the adult both welcomes and fears – will interfere more actively than before in the adult's life. He will force him to pay attention even when the adult may not want to, and will no longer give him the choice, as he did before, of paying him attention or ignoring him. As the relationship grows more antagonistic, the parents' authoritarianism is stimulated. It is a very different thing dealing with a baby who can be confined to his cot, playpen or pram, always caged in and under control, and dealing with a child who rushes around the house touching everything, and whose capacity for movement enables him to escape more and more often and with ever greater success from the impositions of the adult.

From this moment, open conflict breaks out. The mother begins to recognise the child as a threat to her authority, to her desire for order, control and discipline. Their relationship becomes a continual battle. But while the mother allows, or even inwardly wants her son to fight with her and get the better of her because it is in the 'natural order of things' (as it is for her to be defeated), she will not allow the girl to fight and will stamp out any of her pretensions to autonomy. She herself has been denied this autonomy and needs to take her revenge on someone, somehow.

Still less does the mother tolerate competition from someone who is like herself but is not her equal. It is at this point that pitiless, direct and thorough repression begins. Conflict itself need not appear at all with calmer, quieter girls who make less firm, less open demands for independence. On the contrary, great harmony seems to exist between mother and daughter. Apparently, they walk hand in hand, but this idyll is established and maintained wholly at the expense of the daughter.

These are the meek, docile girls, the mother's pets, the tame monkeys, the precocious little ladies pathologically dependent on the mother and always clinging to her. The mother will insist that she has never had any difficulty with such girls because they always respond effortlessly to her expectations: apart from the fact that they refuse to go to the nursery, cry piteously in the mother's absence, do not get on well with other children and are afraid of the slightest thing. In such cases open conflict often does not appear even in adolescence. The girl develops without traumas, leaning on her mother and resembling her perfectly. She will only detach herself, and that with great suffering, when she eventually gets married. Even then she will run to her mother with the slightest problem, excluding her husband from this umbilical tie and living out her relationship with him like the immature little girl that she is.

This kind of repression, whether mild or severe, would tend to make girls rebel violently against their mothers much more often than they do, were it not for two psychological factors which inevitably lead girls back to their parents.

The first is *imitation*. The child learns many things by imitation, though he can also learn by trial and error. Language, for example, is learnt through imitation, while how to open and close a door is generally learnt by repeated attempts and correction of errors. Language is a good illustration of the level of attentiveness and perfect imitation a child can achieve. He is able to imitate the slightest shades of the language that he hears spoken and to reproduce sounds and accents with astonishing exactness. When the parents speak in a different accent from the local one, the child starts by imitating the parents' accent and then turns his attention to the accent and language of the people outside the family, but without ceasing to imitate his family. Into the accent and language which he hears used, the child introduces his own variations in use of words and construction of sentences, thus creating his own personal slang.

The child's imitation of other kinds of behaviour follows a similar pattern. First he imitates the person with whom he is in closest contact. Later he uses other models yet without ceasing to imitate the first, and he introduces personal variations which stem from his uniqueness as an individual. In this way, any child, boy or girl, who is given a doll or puppet will hold it to his breast as he has seen his mother do. The intervention of the adult, however, will aim at differentiating the boy's imitation from the girl's. The girl will be given a doll to nurse and encouraged to do so, while a boy will be discouraged by being given a teddy bear or other vaguely human animal without being taught to nurse it. Nursing a doll is an unequivocally maternal act, the quintessential expression of the female rôle, and is therefore encouraged in girls. Holding an animal which does not resemble a human baby in one's arms is interpreted instead as a manifestation of tenderness and affection in a wider sense and is therefore tolerated even in a boy as long as he is small enough.

Some mothers who are particularly aware of the conditioning into male and female rôles which children undergo from birth and who are determined to change these rôles avoid giving dolls to their daughters, preferring instead to offer them cloth animals. It is not, however, that dolls should be taken away from little girls, but that they should also be offered to boys. In the same way fathers should look after babies of both sexes far more, from their very first days, in order to give the children a realistic and in no way shocking view of the effective interchangeability of father's and mother's rôles, and to offer them a model of male tenderness. Hope for the enrichment of the individual does not lie in disciplining and reducing feminine affection in the way that masculine emotion has been reduced, mutilated, and forbidden to express itself freely – as if men were not moved, did not feel compassion, did not weep or despair. It is not by being forced to compete with or imitate boys that little girls will be offered something more. It is rather by respecting and favouring the choices of each person, regardless of their sex, and by offering less limited, freer models than the prevailing stereotypes that we can ensure that each person realises himself to the full, without having to sacrifice some valid and precious part of himself.

This capacity for imitation is greatest in the first years of life and decreases progressively with age. But while imitation reproduces, through observation, an attitude or way of behaving, until repetition makes the imitation perfect, *identification* goes much deeper. It is a 'psychological process through which a subject assimilates an aspect, property or attribute of another person and totally or partially transforms himself according to that model. Personality constitutes and differentiates itself through a series of identifications'.[6] Through this strongly emotionally oriented process the child absorbs, interiorises and repeats the fundamental models transmitted by his culture. Freud states that, 'Identification is almost the only principle of learning which we need in order to explain the development of personality.'[7] 'Identification operates in a subtle manner,' comments Allport.

To identify with another means to feel oneself to be the other. While at an early stage, boys and girls both identify with the mother, later the boy will identify with the father. The male and female models are so different from one another that to identify oneself with one of the two inevitably produces differentiation. If the division of rôles between the two sexes were not so clear, if the personalities of the parents were not so opposed, then the cross-identification of the boy with his mother and of the girl with her father – which the child might instinctively choose as being right and preferable for establishing the best emotional relationship, either because of an affinity of temperament or because of the absence of one of the two parents – might have less dramatic consequences. If men and women were more alike, and if the social value attributed to the female sex was equal to that attributed to the male sex, male identification with the mother would not be considered degrading, nor would the girl's identification with the father be considered an anomaly. Some girls happen to be born with a far more aggressive and 'male' temperament than many boys, while some boys are born with a much gentler and more sensitive temperament than many girls. If the parental models they were offered for identification were not so opposed to each other, and often so different from the child's original temperament, many individual qualities would not have to be irrevocably lost because they were unacceptable in a person of that sex. As Margaret Mead states: [8]

No skill, no special aptitude, no vividness of imagination or precision of thinking would go unrecognised because the child who possessed it was of one sex rather than the other. No child would be relentlessly shaped to one pattern of behaviour, but instead there should be many patterns, in a world that had learned to allow to each individual the pattern which was most congenial to his gifts.

The difference between imitation and identification consists in the fact that imitation is a repetition of behaviour without any emotional implications (a boy who sees another riding a bicycle tries to do this himself); while in identification he is motivated by the emotional tie with the other which makes him want to be like him. Identification structures the child on *someone else's model* and this phenomenon can be a terribly destructive one. The girl, because of her deep emotional tie with her mother and her recognition of her as being the same, is driven to choose her as a model and to reproduce this model faithfully in herself. The mother's behaviour, her reactions, the relationship between the girl and her mother and between the mother and every other member of the family, all indicate the values to which the mother herself responds (through the unconscious process of identification). The essence of the mother penetrates the girl and is absorbed by her. This means that everything depends on what the mother is like. But however exceptional she may be, she remains a woman; a being with lower social value than the man's, for whom tasks of secondary importance are reserved. If this is the model they must interiorise, girls have little reason to rejoice.

Between two and three years of age, the pressure on a little girl is at its peak. From all sides she is driven towards one goal: that of gradually assuming the female rôle which entails a certain type of predetermined behaviour. Pressures in her upbringing grow ever stronger and more exacting. She is impelled to imitate the models around her and to identify with her mother. This is made more efficient at this age by the fact that the girl is now able to understand the language of adults, full of endless precepts about what she 'should do' and 'should not do'. It is not by chance that the greatest conflicts between girls and their mothers appear around the age of eighteen months, when over-active little tomboys begin to be expected to behave in a fashion more appropriate to their sex. Driven from all sides, opposed, punished if she does not conform to the ideal model, divided between her tendency to identify with her mother and her exuberant energy which, far from being spent, pushes her forward and demands an outlet, the girl engages in a fierce struggle with herself and with others. This struggle is a confused and contradictory one. In it precious energies will be vainly lost. The little girl may be a courageous fighter, but she is surrounded by enemies. The disadvantage for a girl as compared to a boy is that the model to which she must conform is always there in the house, available at every moment to be observed and imitated. The mother is constantly present in a plenitude which is later unmasked as a poverty.

Someone who leaves the house and closes the door behind him is clothed in mystery. The exciting question of where he has gone and what he has gone to do immediately arises for those who are excluded from this outside world. Seeing him go out gives rise to a painful envy, but also to an excitement, a tension, a hope for his return and an expectation of what he will bring from this outside world with which he has such a fascinating link. The imagination feeds on his absences. The desire to know more makes one imagine all sorts of fantastic things which might happen to the one who goes out, and only to him, as soon as he has crossed the threshold. Boy and girl envy the father who works: the former with the unmeasured pride of one who knows himself to be like the father and whose turn it will one day be to have the same adventure; the latter, as the excluded observer of something which will never be hers. 'What does your father do?' 'My father works,' answers a boy proudly. 'And your mother?' 'She stays at home.'

Unlike the boy's, the world of the girl is there in the house with her mother. Everything here is without mystery and without charm: a series of miserable domestic tasks endlessly repeated, the results of which soon disappear so that they have to be started all over again, always the same, rigidly restricting the imagination, dull, frustrating and solitary. And always in the service of others. These rituals, totally devoid of mystery, are carried out before the little girl's eyes and her infantile imagination at first manages to colour and embroider them to the point where her enormous drive to engage in sensory activity induces her to imitate and reproduce her mother's actions. (This also happens with little boys, but this stage soon passes.) While at first her efforts to help her mother will be rejected because she is considered incapable, later they will be demanded of her as a duty, an apprenticeship to her future function as a woman capable of serving the family and society.

The case of little Laura is symptomatic of this. When I started to observe her and take notes on her the child was nineteen months old. Strong, energetic, extremely active, curious about everything and very sociable, she went to a nursery where she had an excellent relationship with the assistant. Her relationship with her mother, who had not wanted her, had apparently been good until the girl had started to walk, but had later become tense and difficult owing to the child's liveliness. The mother was obsessively careful of her person and her house. She would not tolerate the slightest trace of dirt or the slightest stain either in her house, or on herself, or on the girl. The child was scolded if she dirtied her clothes, her knees, her hands or her face, and sometimes she was punished and shut in her room without supper if she came back dirty from the nursery or from a walk. The mother's obsession with cleanliness unleashed violent reactions when the child wet or soiled her pants. The mother accused her of carelessness, of doing it on purpose, of being filthy, and would beat her. Sometimes, when the girl was left longer than usual in her cot while the mother was busy with her phobias of cleanliness, she would soil her pants, and, as she was bored, she would play with her faeces, scattering them all over the place. On these occasions the mother's reaction was extremely violent. She had marked feeding problems, eating very little at meals and preferring to pick at something between mealtimes.

In spite of her fraught relationship with her mother, who demanded an impossible standard of perfection from her, the child managed to achieve a certain calmness at the nursery where she spent a large part of the day and was very active. However, she would persecute smaller children with shoves, kicks, and sometimes bites on the hands and cheeks. She would approach the very small children, coaxing them with a captivating smile, and would hug and kiss them, but as soon as she thought herself unobserved she would bite them, provoking cries of pain and then saying 'Poor thing, he's hurt himself'. At the nursery she was not scolded for this. Efforts were made to distract her with activities which would interest her, while at the same time helpless victims were shielded from her attacks.

The little girl would become extremely agitated whenever another child in the nursery soiled his pants, and would run to tell the assistant and scold the guilty child in turn. Obviously imitating her mother's reaction to her own faeces, she would pull her face into a thousand expressions of disgust, and say 'How revolting!' When she soiled her own pants she would run to the teacher to be changed and although the latter would not make the same type of comment on her accident, she could not rest until she felt herself to be perfectly clean. In the street she was very attracted to dogs' messes. She would crouch down and look at them for a long time, often trying to touch them or even pick them up to take home. It was difficult to stop her doing this or to take her away from such things, which obviously fascinated her.

At the nursery she concentrated a great deal on playing with plasticine. To mitigate the anxiety aroused in her by her inability to hold back her faeces and let people know of the immediacy of her need, and by the punishments that her mother would give her for this, an attempt was made at the nursery to show her how to make shapes out of plasticine which would be like faeces, and to tell her 'This is Laura's pooh.' At first the little girl was delighted, repeating several times 'This is Laura's pooh.' But she didn't dare touch them and got the teacher to touch them instead. She seemed to get a great deal of relief from this episode. She intensified her play with plasticine and wet sand and seemed to form a stronger link with the assistant who had shown this understanding of her problems. During this period there was a marked lessening of her aggression towards smaller children. But the problems with her mother continued, the latter becoming more demanding all the time. She made the child clean up whatever she had dirtied, pick up anything she dropped, tidy up any mess she made, sit still, sleep longer than she needed, keep herself clean, and would not allow her to use any bad language, to shout, or hit other children. In spite of all this Laura continued to be full of enthusiasm and curiosity about everything and everybody. She had made friends with two mechanics who had a car-repair business near her house, and she would spend hours watching them work, asking endless questions. She loved cars and would play with a hammer and nails, pieces of wood, and nuts and bolts, and would fill her pockets with these. At twenty-two months she addressed men (for whom she had a definite preference) correctly, calling them 'mister', and calling women 'Madame'. She knew she was a girl and was able to express this in words. She knew, having seen them, that boys have penises and had been very curious and excited about this, but her curiosity soon passed.

At twenty-two months her behaviour began to change. Having up till this time been a tomboy, or rather an undifferentiated individual, she now began to show certain mannerisms considered typical of girls. She would sit in front of the mirror to comb her hair, and whereas previously she had often brushed her hair energetically without taking any pleasure in her own appearance, she now began to mimic an expression of complacency such as she had evidently seen used by her mother or the assistant. She would raise her eyebrows, bat her eyelids, smile at herself, look at herself in side-view, and bring her face nearer to and further from the mirror so as to see herself better. Some time later she arrived at the nursery with her nails painted and showed them to everybody with great pride. She became more affected. She began to want people to notice her shoes and clothes. At the nursery she had always gone in for such so-called practical everyday activities as washing and cleaning little tables, tiles, varnished doors and floors, but when she did these activities common to all the children in the nursery, she did them in a way all of her own, rapid, improvised, without any special rituals. At a certain moment she introduced into these activities new elements which imitated certain actions of the mother. She started using gestures which had never been hers, but which were typical of her mother. This feminising of herself, using her mother as model, became even more evident when one day she began to clean a table-top and then the door-jamb with a soapy rag. Up until now she had always used generous, careless movements and would not try to get things perfectly clean but just enjoyed the activity for its own sake. But from this day on she adopted precise, inhibited and obsessive movements, just like her mother's in every way. She searched for near-invisible stains and traces of dirt, passing the rag over the same spot again and again until the last trace disappeared. Her lips were compressed and her brow wrinkled with anxiety. She had been invaded by her mother's phobic perfectionism and pathological love of cleanliness.

At the same time Laura's behaviour changed in other ways. Up till then, when bigger children attacked her she had always defended herself with determination and without fear, but now she stopped defending herself and began to endure attacks passively. One day (for the first time) she cried without retaliating when a child hit her. From that day on she adopted this victim's stance more and more, except for her aggression towards the smaller children which continued unchanged. Even here her behaviour could be directly ascribed to imitation of her mother's behaviour, since the mother would often cry over nothing. Whereas before Laura's tears had been angry and did not last long, her crying now became prolonged, as though the girl were taking pleasure in it. She became less active, less daring, calmer, and more apathetic and melancholy. There it was: she had become a little girl. Her behaviour could be categorised as female. She had been tamed, The stereotypes had triumphed.

I have had occasion in many other cases to observe the gradual development – from the age of two and up – of little girls away from an aggression directed at others towards an aggression directed at themselves.

I will cite here the case of two little sisters, one three and a half years old, the other about two. The first time I saw them, the elder was exhibiting auto-aggressive behaviour. If she was annoyed or attacked, she did not defend herself, but would burst into loud crying and start pulling her hair and scratching her face, and as her access of impotent rage grew the child would throw herself on the ground and roll about beating her head against the floor. She would be racked by sobs and then would slowly calm down. These fits would leave her exhausted, apathetic and terribly sad and depressed.

The younger sister up to the age of about twenty-two months had a completely different attitude. She would attack other children with a hard, hostile expression on her tense little face, and would keep up the attacks until the other child started to cry. At this point she would stop with an air of triumph. If by chance someone dared to attack her, her reaction was immediate and violent even if the other child was stronger than herself. He would of course get the better of her, but she didn't care: she would grit her teeth and renew the attack. Gradually her behaviour started to change and to become more like her sister's, until they were almost identical. She no longer reacted to aggression with aggression but instead would throw herself to the ground and cry, refusing to be consoled or helped. She would take refuge in a corner, sad and disconsolate, in a mood of self-pity. The mother of these girls was obviously the model that both had imitated and identified with. Discontented, easily moved to tears, rough with other children, she rejected any suggestion as to how she might improve her difficult family situation. Although she deprecated it loudly she would do nothing to get herself out of it. One after the other the daughters had reproduced her behaviour at the moment when the process of identification had been set into motion.

Direct interventions

It is like a concerted attack from all sides: imitation of the adult, the more significant identification with the adult, and direct interventions during upbringing. Everything drives the child in the same direction: whether he imitates adults generally, or whether he identifies himself with a specific adult, he finds adult models which conform perfectly to the stereotyped values of our culture.

I report here word for word an example of a banal conversation between a mother and daughter which contains all the elements we have mentioned: imitation and identification can be seen in several instances (the little bag, the mirror, mimicking, gestures which are identical to those of the mother, etc.). The direct educational interventions are so typical as to need no comment.

The Context – The mother comes with her twenty-six-month-old girl to talk to me about her. She complains about some things that are not going well, and she cites these in order of importance:

– The little girl was placed for ten days in a nursery in a convent, but her mother had had to stay with her because she cried as soon as the mother began to leave. After ten days, the mother ceased to bring her child to the nursery because she seemed to be suffering too much. The mother admitted that she too suffered from the experience. She had no intention of renewing the attempt, even in a better nursery, until the following year.

– The child is aggressive with other children. She doesn't want

L.G.—.3

to play with them and bites them if they approach her. Her mother scolds her for this and takes her away from the other children.

– The girl still wets her pants sometimes. Her mother gets very annoyed by this. She was told by some women in the park that their children had been using the pot since the age of eight or nine months. Why couldn't hers do this?

– The child hardly eats anything; she allows herself to be fed but keeps the food in her mouth for hours, and yet she is very healthy and her weight is perfectly normal. How can she get her to eat more?

– The child sleeps 13 hours a night and two hours in the day; but this suits her fine because she can get some peace.

– The mother would like to resolve these problems in a week to fifteen days at most.

The Action – She comes in holding the little girl tightly by the hand, although there is no danger in sight. We ask the little one to sit down on a small two-seat sofa designed for children. A table is placed before her and she is offered a box full of plastic shapes to thread into a necklace. The little girl is quite happy with this and starts to help herself, completely absorbed in her play. The mother is annoyed that the girl is immersed in playing because it stops her from showing how well she has brought her up, that is to say how obedient she is. Here begins a disturbingly revealing scene which shows the 'gentle' inflexible repression to which the girl is being subjected.

Conversation – The mother turns to her daughter with the mewing tone that almost everyone uses with children and a fixed artificial smile, by definition a 'feminine' pose.

Mother: Betta, do you want to take your coat off?

Betta: (doesn't answer but smiles)

Mother: Do you want to keep your coat on?

Betta: Yes.

Mother: That's a nice game, isn't it?

Betta: (doesn't answer but smiles)

Mother: Then you don't want to take your coat off?

Betta: (doesn't answer but smiles)

Mother: Shall Mummy take your coat off?

Betta: (doesn't answer)

Mother: If you feel like weeing, tell Mummy.

Betta: Yes.

Mother: (jumping up and leaning over the child) Come and I'll take you to do a wee-wee.

Betta: (shakes her head) Don't feel like it.

Mother: Are you sure you don't feel like it?

Betta: (doesn't answer)

Mother: Be careful you don't drop the toys on the floor.

Betta: (doesn't answer)

Mother: So you like that game, do you?

Betta: Yes.

Meanwhile I walk in front of Betta who raises her eyes to look at me and smiles.

Betta: Where are you going?

I: To the toilet to do wee-wee. (This is quite true.)

Betta: (smiles interestedly)

I: (coming out of the bathroom) Can I sit next to you?

Betta: (nods happily and moves to make room for me; we do not speak but look at each other in silence and like each other)

Mother: Who is this lady?

Betta: (does not answer but looks at me and smiles)

Mother: Do you like the lady?

Betta: Yes. (And smiles openly at me)

Mother: Have you told the lady your name?

Betta: (does not answer)

Mother: Why don't you show the lady your little bag?

Betta: (shows the bag)

Mother: What have you got in your bag, Betta?

Betta: A mirror.

Short pause.

Mother: Will you tell the lady your name?

Betta: (says nothing)

Mother: Why won't you tell the lady what you are called?

Betta: (says nothing)

Mother: This lady's nice, isn't she?

Betta: (says nothing)

Mother: (turning to me) Strange, she's such a chatterbox usually, you know. (Turning to Betta) You know the toys belong to this lady?

Betta: (looks at me in silence)

Mother: Don't put your foot on top of the other, Betta, you'll spoil your new shoes

Betta: (obeys)

Mother: Have you told this lady how old you are?

Betta: (making a sign with her fingers) Two.

I: You're a big girl, then.

Mother: Yes, but this girl still does wee-wee in her pants sometimes!

I: (pretend not to have heard)

Mother: Do you feel like weeing, Betta?

Betta: No.

Mother: Do you want your tea now?

Betta: (shakes her head)

Mother: You're keeping your coat on then?

Betta: (says nothing)

This bombardment has gone on for only a few minutes, but everything leads one to suppose that Betta's days are studded with such maternal interventions, as well as those of her grandmother with whom she is often left.

The conversation reported above is typical in the sense that it could not have taken place between a mother and son. The parents have fixed in their minds a very precise model to which the children must conform according to sex. Through a set of innumerable spoken precepts, the adult transmits to the child the values to which he must conform on pain of social unacceptability. These laws are reinforced by the child's own peer group. The other children have also heard them from their parents and in their turn want them to be respected.

The whole process of upbringing seems to revolve around this differentiation, and the demands the adult makes on the child always bears its imprint. Let us give a series of random examples of these differentiated requirements. We disapprove of a girl learning to whistle, but it seems natural for a boy to. We intervene if a girl laughs coarsely, but it is all right if a boy does. We don't tolerate a girl being untidy, but it seems natural for a boy. A girl is expected not to shout or talk in a loud voice, but in a boy it seems natural. We punish a girl, looking horrified if she uses rude words, but if a boy uses the same words it only provokes laughter. If a boy doesn't say please and thank you we make excuses for him, but if a girl does not say it we get very annoyed. If a boy refuses to go and get something for us we regard him as being within his rights and we go and get it ourselves, but if a girl refuses it seems like an open rebellion. We tolerate a boy interrupting grown-up conversation far more than a girl. We allow a boy to have bad table manners but we expect good behaviour from a girl. If a little girl is unkind to smaller children she seems monstrously wicked to us, but we expect a boy to ill-treat them rather than cuddle or kiss them. If a boy takes something from another child we stop him, but we really expect him to act like this, whereas we expect a girl not to. If a girl ill-treats her cat or dog we think this is the depths of depravity but we think it quite normal in a boy. We ridicule a boy who is afraid, but not a girl. If a girl whines we tell her that it is boring, but we pay her attention; if a boy does it we tell him he is a cissy. We encourage boys to play war games, to climb trees, and to build themselves up physically, but we prevent girls from doing the same things. If a girl kicks a ball we teach her that it is better to throw it by hand, but we teach a boy that it is better to kick it. We are irritated by an untidy girl who gets dirty and tears her clothes, but we accept it from a boy. If a girl refuses unwanted offers of help in overcoming some difficulty, we help her all the same, but a boy who refuses is admired for already being such a little man. If a boy pretends to smoke we laugh, but if a girl does it, it seems distasteful. If we find a boy playing with his genitals we tell him to stop, but if we find a girl doing it, then not only do we tell her to stop, we also show our disgust.

The list could go on forever. The adult quite automatically selects the type of intervention according to sex. During a visit I paid to the mother of a boy and a girl who were very close in age, she asked the boy to open the garage door so that I could put my car in, and she asked the girl to bring me a glass of milk. Would she ever have asked the girl to open the garage for me or the boy to bring me a glass of milk? The adult chooses which orders to give which child according to a code of which he is not conscious, but which is related to the law that the jobs which are more important, or at least which are considered as such, should be entrusted to the male. Both children were certainly just as capable of opening the garage door as of fetching a glass of milk, but in this case the more 'masculine' task had been chosen for one and the more 'feminine' task for the other. The children themselves probably would not have obeyed so readily if the orders had been the other way round, because they had already been conditioned to categorise and recognise tasks as being appropriate to one or the other sex.

We're still on about penis envy

'I've got one and you haven't' is an anatomical fact which cannot be disputed. But it is arguable whether 'penis envy' is an element of feminine psychology which has its roots in anatomical differences, as modern psychoanalysis maintains, or whether it has its roots in social differences instead. In other words, do girls envy boys because they have penises, or because, being possessors of penises, they enjoy numerous privileges which are denied to girls. Eibl-Eibesfeldt says:

> While recognising the merits of psychoanalysis on this point [that part of upbringing which psychoanalysis describes as sexual] one must all the same accuse certain of its exponents of unscientific methods; plausible hypotheses are too readily assumed to be explicable on grounds of cause, and tend to be based on the Oedipus complex, fear of castration, and penis envy in girls, as though one were dealing with proven facts. But in fact nothing is proven. It is true that in certain cases a girl wishes to be a boy, or a son experiences conflicts with his father at an early age, but these can be explained outside the sexual field, and just as plausibly, as conflicts of rank.[9]

While many little girls discover the anatomical differences between themselves and boys early on, there are others who have never had the opportunity and yet they already clearly realise the social superiority of the male, and, by contrast, their own inferiority. They don't even have to deduce this fact from the relationship between themselves and their peers. It is more than enough for them to see what happens within the family. It is not difficult for a girl to deduce from her father's authority at home, from the regard in which he is held by her mother and other relations, from the work which her father does outside the home, and from the economic dependence of his relations on him, which continue even when the woman is earning more, that it is men who really count. The comparison between the consideration given to girls and that given to their male counterparts will confirm what they have seen so far. At the moment when they discover the anatomical difference which consists of that 'something more' that they don't have, they will draw the obvious conclusion, and will deduce that those who have a penis also have prestige and authority. And if they have already discovered this anatomical difference they will have started from another point but still arrive at the same conclusion.

Even if the girl has a mother who dominates her husband, she will still realise that her dominant rôle is limited to the narrow confines of the family. Outside the family, even a dominant wife holds a subservient position in relation to the most dominated of men. Nobody likes to discover that he or she is regarded as a second-class individual. This discovery causes suffering, weakens self-esteem, diminishes ambition, limits self-realisation and arouses envy for the privileged and a desire to be like them. Continuous confrontation with boys who are benefiting from the privileges which have been denied to girls makes the latter lose a considerable amount of the self-esteem which is indispensable for realising their objectives and for fighting their own battles. Girls and women in fact suffer from a much greater sense of inferiority than do men. The greater the insecurity or doubt about one's value, the greater is the anxiety about adapting oneself to the approved model and the greater the effort one makes to understand what is required of one in order to live up to others' expectations. The more successful one is in adapting to the approved model, the more certainty one has of being loved and accepted.

Little boys also make this discovery.

For children, the body is an essential point of reference. They cannot imagine that another body might be different from theirs and the discovery fills them with astonishment until they have assimilated it. Hence their desire for verification. The discovery can also upset a child profoundly, but only for the short time it takes for him to accept it, as he has previously accepted and will later accept many other important discoveries.

The discovery of anatomical differences between the sexes is comparable to discovering differences in skin colour. The child who meets a black man for the first time is strongly marked by the encounter. But he quickly and easily adjusts to the discovery because it is not reinforced by social attitudes which assign a superior rôle to the black race. But the black child when he discovers the existence of white people – for whom power is reserved and who have a social value far higher than his own – will feel 'white man envy', at least in those countries where his own social inferiority is a constant problem. White skin, like the penis, becomes the symbol of power and therefore an object of envy.

When little girls make the discovery that they have 'something less' than boys, nobody reassures them about the value of their own sex, because nobody believes in it. The father does not believe it and the mother even less. Men don't believe it, but neither do women. Among women there is none of that proud sexual solidarity that exists among men. While 'we men' has the triumphant ring of those who belong to a privileged group, 'we women' has the self-recriminatory tone of the oppressed. A girl's discovery that she has not got a penis is not compensated for by anything else. I have seen a little girl of three jumping with joy and running to tell teacher and friends in the nursery that an assistant had assured her that she had equally important things, when the little girl had protested that she lacked a penis! No woman, except for so-called 'deviants', seriously wishes to be male and have a penis. But most women would like to have the privileges and the opportunities that go with it. Psychoanalysis has succeeded in making women feel guilty of failed femininity if they obstinately refuse to be considered as second-class individuals. The absence of penis envy should in fact, according to psychoanalysts, distinguish the really 'feminine' women, that is, those perfectly adapted to and satisfied with their condition. In other words, the only real women would be those who had happily accepted their position of inferiority which is a decidedly masculine point of view.

Dr. Bernard Muldworf says:

> It is not the absence of a penis which makes a woman unhappy, it is her secondary place in social production. But this secondary rôle instead of being attributed to its real cause – an organisation of society which divides the community into antagonistic classes – is actually attributed to nature or biology which do not constitute the origin of social production but are on the contrary transformed and directed by it.[10]

Notes

1 Reported by J. Chasseguet Smirgel, op. cit.
2 Robert Stoller, quoted by Shulamith Firestone in *The Dialectic of Sex*, Jonathan Cape, London 1971.
3 René Zazzo, *L'evoluzione del fanciullo dai 2 ai 6 anni* in Maurice Debesse, *Psicologia dell'età evolutiva*, Armando, Rome 1968, p. 64.
4 Charles Bried, *Gli e scolari e le scolare*, in Maurice Debesse, op. cit., p. 341.
5 Irenaus Eibl-Eibesfeldt, *Amore e odio*, Adelphi, Milan 1971, p. 69.

6   Jean Laplanche and J.-B. Pontalıs, *Vocabulaire de la psychoanalyse*, P.U.F., Paris 1971.
7   Gordon W. Allport, op. cit.
8   Margaret Mead, op. cit., p. 321.
9   Irenaus Eibl-Eibesfeldt, op. cit., p 200
10 Bernard Muldworf, *Fémininité et psychologie féminine selon la psychoanalise* in 'Bulletin Officiel de la Société Française de Psycho-Prophilaxie', Paris 1964.

Chapter 3

GAMES, TOYS AND CHILDREN'S LITERATURE

> 'Mum says she won't buy me a broom.'
> 'And why won't she buy you one?'
> 'Because I'm a boy.'
> *Dialogue between a boy of two and a half and an*
> *assistant at the crèche.*

The child's tendency to play games is certainly innate, but the game he chooses, its rules, and the equipment it entails are the products of a culture. A game-playing heritage is passed down from one generation to the next, from adults to children and from older children to younger children, and the variations at each transition are limited.

> Invented games are very rare and ephemeral. Invention is mostly limited to accidental modifications among small children and minor improvements made by older children of twelve upwards. This is the group which provides the rituals of movement or speech. But these rituals mostly originate from adults. One can often find in the past and in primitive tribes the source of games which are now played by our children.[1]

When adults assert that it is the child himself who chooses what game he will play, they are ignoring the fact that before he can show a preference for one game or another, he must have learnt the games themselves from somebody else. And that somebody else must already have made a choice in his turn from the range of materials available for play, whether re-usable or disposable. In other words, games and toys are the products of a particular culture which permits choices to be made which appear to have ample scope, but which are in fact very limited. In this domain, differentialism based on sex is particularly evident. Most of the toys one finds in shops are geared towards the stereotyped rôles one expects little boys and little girls to fulfil.

The problem of knowing which toys to give children from the tenderest age onwards is a major one. Since children are unable to hold objects in their hand until four or five months, up until then the adult concentrates on visual stimuli.

We have already spoken of the different ways in which the baby's room is decorated. Fairly recent is the use of mobiles to hang in the baby's room. These may be made of paper, light wood, metal or plastics, and are attached to metal hangers which are suspended from nylon threads and move easily in the slightest draught, attracting and holding the baby's attention: birds, animals, abstract forms, boats, flowers, sailing ships, etc. I have often been present at the choosing of these objects which provide very good visual stimuli for babies from six weeks onwards, and I have noticed that the choice tends to be made on the basis of two fundamental requirements: the bright colour of the objects and what they represent. Although colour did not present any problems as far as the baby's sex was concerned, apart from the notorious pink which is banned for boys, the objects represented gave rise to innumerable considerations. Yachts, ships, canoes, cars, horses and abstract shapes in various colours and forms were chosen only for boys. Birds, ducks, swans, fish, chickens, circus animals, balloons and coloured geometrical forms were chosen equally for either sex, while flowers, angels, snowflakes and dolls were chosen only for girls. The provocative suggestion that one buy a girl a mobile representing, say, a naval flotilla, was always turned down energetically, and the explanation given for these refusals was quite simple and sure: it was not suitable for a girl.

The various teething-rings, rattles and little things which are given to the baby to hold or are hung over his cradle respect the laws of pink and blue. When it comes to rubber or rag dolls or soft toys, the selection becomes even stricter. Proper dolls with an unequivocally feminine appearance are reserved for girls while animals are offered to both sexes. Dolls are sometimes also given to boys as long as they are definitely identifiable as male. But baby dolls are forbidden to boys from the earliest age.

When someone gives a doll or a stuffed animal to a little girl, they are not content with just offering it and waiting to see what she will do with it, they also show her how to hold it in her arms and nurse it. This demonstration of 'parental care' is not given to her male contemporaries since nursing babies is not part of the male tradition in manifestations of affection. As a result, one sees girls of ten or eleven months who have already acquired the conditioned reflex to doll-nursing and as soon as one gives them a doll or a soft toy they hold it to their breasts and rock it to sleep. Adults, forgetting that this behaviour is only the result of their teaching, exclaim at the biological miracle; so little and she already has the maternal instinct! It fills them with joy because the phenomenon is seen as a reassuring sign of normality. It is very curious to observe how boys of the same age who are not trained like the girls hold the same dolls in their arms in a far more casual way; upright instead of lying horizontally or with an arm round their neck squeezing them or even crushing their heads. In any case, they hardly ever nurse them.

It is fairly common at bedtime for children to ask to be allowed to keep a doll or teddy bear or some other soft toy towards which they feel particular affection. While girls are often permitted to take a doll to bed, it is rare for a boy to be allowed to do so. If they really want to have a companion in bed, whether it is a doll or an animal, it must be of their sex. Later, girls are made to go on because this play is considered to be really good training for their future maternal function, while a boy who shows preference for this sort of play will be discouraged and pushed into more aggressive and competitive types of games.

When a boy wants to play with dolls in a mixed group of boys and girls this is tolerated, because in this way he can assume the rôles of father, husband, or son, which are recognised and approved of as masculine. 'Let's pretend that I'm the father and you're the mother', or perhaps 'Let's say that I'm the baby and you're the mother'. In this extremely liberating game, dolls are scolded, ill-treated, smacked and punished. In other words they are given the same prohibitive treatment that the children get from their parents. Up till the age of five or six both boys and girls love games which imitate household activities. They have a strong desire to take part in mother's domestic activities which are fascinating because of the materials involved: water, fire and food. Vegetables, for example, which are washed and then diced, sliced, minced or puréed change their appearance and consistency with cooking and are then drained, stirred, mixed and seasoned. All this constitutes a stimulating and enjoyable experience for children. A girl at that age passes, without realising it, from imitative games to really sharing in the mother's household duties, and is happy and proud to be asked to help to her full capacity, while still being allowed an element of play. But a boy gradually rejects this kind of play until he drops it completely from his repertoire.

It is after the age of five or six that the paths of the two sexes diverge completely. While boys now view housework with scorn, girls are brought back to it by the strength of their identification with their mother and by her need for help. Reminders of their future duties, of the children they will have, of their home and of the husband they will have to look after, will be repeated continuously and persuasively, as if it were sensed that if girls were left free they would despise domestic work as much as boys do. So it is not simply a question of an apprenticeship aimed at learning certain abilities, but of real conditioning undertaken with the aim of making sure that certain services are provided automatically. In fact, if this were not the intention of adults, a few months of intensive tuition before marriage would be all that was necessary for a girl to learn how to run a home. Housework is so banal that anyone can learn it in a very short time. But adults know very well that if conditioning is not carried out at the right age – that is at an age when criticism and rebellion are unlikely to occur – it will be all the harder to obtain these services later on. Social and family conventions demand that women consent to submit to the job of domestic servants, for their refusal would put in jeopardy both the male caste which has been conditioned to being served, and the entire social structure which refuses to bear the costs of female domestic labour or the cost of introducing some substitute.

Good and bad toys

Toy merchants know very well that anyone who buys a toy as a present always has the child's sex in mind. To the typical request 'I would like a toy suitable for a child of two' they will generally reply, 'Is it for a boy or a girl?' It is true that there are some neutral toys, that is, toys considered suitable for children of either sex. These are generally unstructured materials – like the infinite variety of constructional toys, mosaics, puzzles; modelling materials such as plasticine, etc.; crayons and paints; musical instruments, although such instruments as trumpets are regarded as purely masculine; and so on. However, as soon as the toys consist of perfectly identifiable and structured elements sexual differentiation becomes clear. For girls there is a large range of toys which consists of miniaturised household fittings, such as kitchen and toilet sets; nurses' bags equipped with thermometers, bandages, sticking plasters and syringes, interiors of rooms such as bathrooms, bedrooms, babies' rooms; outfits to sew and embroider, irons, tea-services, electrical appliances, prams, baths and endless dolls with their outfits. Toys for boys are completely different: vehicles for land, sea and air, transport of all shapes and sizes, warships, aircraft carriers, nuclear missiles, spaceships, weapons of all kinds from perfect replicas of cowboy pistols to sinister-looking machine guns which differ from the real thing only by virtue of their greater safety, swords, scimitars, bows and arrows, and cannons; a real military arsenal.

Between these two groups of toys there is no place for choice or even concession. Even the parent most anxious to follow the inclinations and desires of the child in his choice of toys will not accede to a request for a machine gun for a girl or a tea-set for a boy. It would be impossible for him, he would consider it sacrilege. In any case, the differentiation that is imposed on boys and girls is such that 'peculiar' tastes in toys after the age of four or five really signify that the child has not accepted his or her sexual rôle and that therefore something has gone wrong. Even when it is a question of 'neutral' toys, that is, those suitable for children of either sex, the fact that they are intended for use more by males than females, or vice versa, is often obvious from the illustrations on the box or packaging. Typical of this are the plastic 'Lego' bricks on whose boxes only boys are depicted building skyscrapers, towers, armoured cars, houses, etc. Lego, however, also sell special boxes of bricks for girls in which, just for a change, are the components for constructing complete kitchen fittings, including refrigerators, washing machines, and washing-up machines; or drawing-rooms, bathrooms, bedrooms and so on. Obviously in this case the picture of a boy on the box gives way to that of a girl, the future wife/mother/consumer.

For some time the packets of a well-known brand of crisps have had on them a stylised drawing of a girl and a label saying 'for girls'. The back of the packet explains: 'Girls! this product contains a surprise gift. Inside you will find dolls, cutlery, pots and pans, hairslides, bracelets, rings, powder-compacts, combs, irons, dolls, and many other delightful toys'. The two basic elements of a girl's upbringing are perfectly respected in this list of toys: running the house and the care of her appearance. On the corresponding packet for boys it said: 'Boys! This product contains a surprise gift. Inside you may find: soldiers, aeroplanes, armoured cars, kits for making model vintage cars and ships, spinning tops, cap pistols, whistles, little trains, badges of football teams, and many many other lovely toys.' All in order as one can see.

Parents maintain that children spontaneously choose toys which are suitable for their sex, thereby showing very precise tendencies. It is fairly common for a boy in front of a shop window to demand that his parents buy him a car, aeroplane or gun, until he is hysterical. Often the parents refuse him, producing various reasons (that it costs too much, he already has lots etc), but not that they consider it unsuitable for him. The boy's fixation establishes itself therefore on the certainty that it is a *permitted* toy and comes after a whole series of offers of exactly that type of toy, and an equally long series of refusals to requests for other sorts of toys. The obstinacy of the child in insisting on that particular toy is nothing but a final pseudo-choice between the choices which have already been made by the adults. The adult, in fact, will give in sooner or later to the child's requests, but it is very rare for an adult to give in when the child tries to insist on something which is considered unsuitable. I heard a boy of about five who was following his mother round the supermarket insist all the way round that his mother buy him some soap for doing the washing. 'But when can I do the washing?' the child kept asking insistently. 'You can't do the washing,' answered the mother inflexibly, 'you're a boy.' 'But I want to do the washing with soap,' insisted the boy and the mother did not even answer, until the boy went to the shelf, took a piece of soap and put it in the trolley. The mother, furious, put it back and scolded him severely; at this point the child began to weep with rage. But the mother was unmoved. Surely after such a significant and unquestionable refusal that boy will no longer try to ask for washing soap but will orientate his requests towards things which he has learnt to recognise as acceptable.

A young woman told me that she could still remember perfectly the acute sense of guilt she had felt when at the age of seven she had come upon her mother complaining to a friend that she did not like playing with dolls. From that moment on she forced herself to play with them, wanting as she did to comply at all costs with her mother's expectations, to be approved by her and to please her, even though she continued to prefer more active games.

I have often had occasion to observe that in nursery schools where the child is left a free choice of games, toys, and activities, that girls will play with cars, aeroplanes, ships etc., until the age of about three. I have seen girls of 18 or 20 months old spend hours and hours taking a whole lot of little cars, aeroplanes, helicopters, boats and trains from a bag, line them up on a carpet, and move them about with the same pleasure and the same concentration as little boys. In the same way one can see boys spending the whole morning washing, cleaning the tables and polishing shoes. Later this pattern of play disappears. Children have already learnt to ask for the 'right' toy because they know the wrong one will be denied them.

An infant school teacher who is particularly sensitive to these problems told me that when she had brought into the class a toy consisting of nuts, bolts, screwdrivers etc., an excited girl quite pink with joy, took possession of it. As she was heading towards a little table with her newly acquired treasure, a little boy of about four leapt on her and tried to snatch it away from her. The teacher intervened, saying that he could have it later when the girl had finished with it. The boy reacted by saying 'But it's mine, it's a boy's game.' The teacher made it clear that there is no such thing as a boy's game or a girl's game, but that all games are the same and all children can play at them. The boy was astonished. He looked at the teacher as though she were quite mad and hung around the girl for a long time with a deeply perplexed air, revealing the state of mind of one who has assisted at the violation of a law he had believed immutable, and who cannot reconcile himself to it. It would be a good thing if such violations were made more often, whether by parents or by teachers. If the teacher had not made her point of view clear, both children would have received confirmation of what they already knew about toys and all the implications of sexual discrimination in this area. Whereas the little girl would have been humiliated and driven back into a state of inferiority, the boy would have had his superiority confirmed.

Children's games and social reality

Children's games and the way they play with toys reflect more than ever the society in which they live. Charles Bried states:

Some American investigations have made it possible to establish lists of toys classified according to their index of masculinity or femininity. At one extreme of these lists one finds games involving dolls and household activities; at the other are constructional toys *which involve the use of tools, that is, yet again, activities which correspond to the social occupations characteristic of adults of either sex.*[2]

This phenomenon is so obvious that it is astonishing that Erikson should go back to the improbable biological concept of 'internal space' to explain the different ways that a group of girls and boys of ten to 12 years of age used a number of toys chosen at random, when they were invited to construct, one at a time, on a particular table, exciting scenes from an imaginary film. Erikson confesses that even as the game was unfolding before his eyes he realised that he was expecting the boys to construct one kind of scene and the girls an entirely different one. His expectations were very soon confirmed. The girls actually constructed scenes of domestic interiors, generally enclosed in a circle by furniture while the boys constructed exterior scenes with skyscrapers, towers and streets full of traffic and so on. Erikson interprets these different results from boys and girls in a 'genital' way. He sees in the girls' closed scenes a relationship with the 'internal' female organs, and in the boys' open 'external' scenes a relationship with their external erectile organs. It still remains to be shown that girls of ten to 12 are conscious of possessing a vagina, though it is obvious that boys know their genitals and their relative characteristics very well. It also needs to be demonstrated that it really is this unconscious biological 'notion' which influences the children in their scene-building activity. Erikson takes into account, on a secondary level, the social origins of these scenes: the aggressive male motivated towards achieving a high, independent position in the world and the little girls whose representation of house interiors means 'that they are concentrating on the anticipated task of taking care of a home and rearing children.' But his principle thesis remains that of 'spatial' concept which is different for males and females and which depends on their different sexual anatomy. Even the episode of the black child who built his own, equally 'masculine' scene, but under rather than on the table – fails to illuminate him. Erikson comments. 'He thus offers stark and chilling evidence of the meaning of his smiling meekness: he "knows his place".'

The black child knows he is male and at the same time, he knows that he belongs to his race: from his family and his social environment he has received a double message, that is, the fact of there being different rôles for each sex, and the other undeniable fact of his race's inferiority and subordination to white men. The girls with their repeated representation of the interiors of houses where the usual family scenes go on, show that they have understood equally well that that is 'their place'.

Girls and boys, including the little black boy, do nothing but respond to the expectations of adults, including Erikson.

It could also be that between the ages of ten and 12 boys do identify with their 'intrusive and erectile' genital organ, so that they build skyscrapers and towers which resemble it, just as it could be that girls somehow 'know' that they have an internal space called a vagina. It is doubtful, however, that children are more susceptible to these suggestive physiological sensations than they are to the real, universal experience they have of their different rôles: active/external for boys and passive/internal for girls. Girls' games which take place within the four walls of their home are often interrupted, moved or stopped, so that they can help with the housework. This rarely happens to boys, who therefore have more time left to play. While boys grow up with the conviction that they have the right to play, girls are persuaded that they only have the right to play once they have fulfilled their duty, which consists only of making themselves useful. More control in games of movement, greater tidiness, more care not to disturb others: this is generally required of them.

There are, it is true, many families in which various services are also asked of boys. These, however, are generally chosen from tasks considered more suitable for boys, tasks which will not injure their dignity. Boys are asked to help out much less often, and if they refuse, as often happens, they are not made to feel particularly guilty, unlike girls who are often told: 'What will happen when you are grown-up if you won't behave like a little lady now?' The corresponding question: 'What will happen when you are grown-up if you won't behave like a good little man now?' has a totally different meaning. Even if the parents did say it, the good little man is still the one who will go out of the house and earn money to keep his family, not the one who has to help the mother lay the table and wash up.

As soon as performing these tasks ceases to be an attraction and becomes a boring duty, the boy learns tactics to save himself from having to do them, knowing that he will remain unpunished. In fact adults are far more surprised if a boy agrees to help in the house than if he refuses.

The greater respect accorded to boys' play is confounded by a

greater respect for their idleness. So-called idleness i
very often the result of their need, shared by adults, to
over in peace, to give free rein to their imagination, a
up channels of communication with their inner self.
reawakens from these pauses charged with new energy, .y to
launch himself into new experiences. The amount of respect which
an adult has for a child's so-called idleness once again reflects his
differing degree of respect towards the two sexes. Respect for
idleness in boys will continue into adulthood. The moments in
which the man is free from work are sacred for the entire family.
The wife who has worked just as hard and is often more tired than
her husband bends over backwards to make sure his rest is
respected by his children.

Different ways of playing

Male and female do not merely differ in their choice of games
and toys but also as Bried [4] observes, in the way that they play.
More aggression and muscular strength, and a desire for intense
action in boys; a preponderance of verbal aggression, but calmness and stability and a 'predilection for rituals and ceremonies
that later will consolidate themselves into a docile and almost
voluptuous submission to formal restrictions' in girls. No one can
deny that these differences exist and that they are quite evident.
One only has to watch groups of children playing to be convinced
of this. But people keep going back to the 'biological' factor, which
is completely unproved, in order to explain what can be explained
equally plausibly by the 'social' factor.

The way a girl is forced to be less aggressive makes her select an
acceptable way of expressing herself even when she is playing. A
group of little girls acts as a control in itself and a very aggressive girl will find herself left out. We have seen how in play the
diffferences between boys and girls in the first few years are
minimal, but grow ever greater with the passing of time.

We have also noted the reassuring and repetitive rituals which
are the refuge of many girls who have been the objects of massive
repression because of what is considered to be their excessive
vitality, curiosity and energy. The case quoted by Lézine shows the
way that children can react with phobic behaviour to interventions intended to limit their vitality.

Is it not possible that the repetitive, ritualised, restricted games that girls play, in which they concentrate on acquiring refined but limited skills, are really nothing but phobic behaviour based on obsessive ritual? That they are a general aspect of that anxious perfectionism which replaces the aggressiveness that has been repressed and inhibited?

This is typified by group or individual skipping games, which progress from the most elementary – consisting of jumping with feet together – to the most complex which demand skilled coordination of movement – involving such combinations as one jump on the left foot, one jump on the right foot, and two jumps with the feet together, at the same time crossing the rope over one's head. I have seen this done by a girl of about eight who while she was skipping seemed to be in a state of hypnosis. This way of playing with a skipping rope seems to be unknown to boys who won't even try it, scornfully dismissing skipping as being 'for girls'.

Another ritualistic game that girls repeat to the point of obsession is bouncing a ball against a wall. Here too, the variations on the main action – throwing the ball against the wall and catching it – are amazing in their complexity. The ball is passed under the knee, caught only after a pirouette or thrown backwards, all to the accompaniment of some verbal rigmarole. Hopscotch is another girls' game in which the rules are based on delicacy, precision and fine coordination of movement.

It would be easy to attribute little girls' choice of such games to some mysterious and improbable biological root if it were not also found among boys who have identified with a female rather than a male – though they are biologically male – and who therefore imitate feminine behaviour. On the other hand, among girls who are more active, or at least who are allowed more freedom and are used to playing in the open, this type of game is very rare. Then they only engage in such games if they have girls of their own age around them and probably because they want to be accepted by the group. They are less good at these games than the others, though they are very good at 'boys' games such as climbing trees or over gates, playing war or cowboys, running along pretending to drive a car, and so on.

The widespread wearing of trousers from a very young age and the resulting greater freedom of movement has almost certainly made accessible to girls many 'boys' games which until a few years ago were made impossible by skirts which got in the way.

Besides the 'code' of forbidden and permitted behaviour which defines modesty and immodesty has changed considerably. If a girl was wearing a skirt and sat with her legs apart, it would be considered decidedly indecent unless she was very small, while the same posture is quite acceptable in trousers. 'Grace', that mysterious emanation of 'biological' femininity, is shown to be as vulnerable as most other aspects of conditioning when social custom suddenly becomes less certain. One often sees girls who are used to wearing trousers adopt the same casual pose when they are wearing a skirt.

But with clothes too, girls can never follow their own inclinations, and know them to be their own. They will always have a different feminine image flashing before their eyes, and however much they try to flee it they will always be forced back towards it in a state of perpetual ambivalence. Thus, girls used to wearing trousers will feel the need to wear a dress which is all frills and frippery in order to feel really feminine – a dress which they will have to be careful not to spoil or dirty, and in which they must behave with circumspection in order to match the air of its flounces.

Movement games

In the day-to-day relationship between adults and children the order 'keep still' is one of the most frequent. For the child it must be completely incomprehensible, since movement does not result from any decision he makes but from an urge as powerful as the urge to eat. It would never occur to anybody to make a child miss his meal, because there is an obvious correlation between food and his physical development. But the relationship between movement and physical and intellectual development is not so obvious. Adults think it strange that children have to pass through such a long stage of restlessness before becoming sedentary beings like themselves. Their lives are so ordered by various rhythms that they suffer the perpetual movement of children with irritation. They would like them to become adults at once, passing from the cradle straight into maturity, that is to maximum immobility. Parents do not have much tolerance of active games. They do not understand them, so they ask children to keep still or play farther away.

Movement requires very fine neuromuscular coordination and intense activity. The more a child moves the more chance he will have to have sensory experiences of his surroundings and the more his brain cells and his intelligence will develop. To reduce his opportunities for movement means reducing his curiosity, his experiences, and hence his intelligence. The child who grows up in an atmosphere poor in stimulus and freedom develops his intellect less than the child who lives in a richer, more varied, and more tolerant atmosphere.

The repression of a child's movement can be interpreted as a refusal to accept him for what he is. It happens more markedly and more consistently with little girls because they have to adhere to the chosen model at all costs. This means that a girl's curiosity and opportunities for having experiences are less often satisfied and less stimulated than a boy's. This creates a mammoth impediment to their use of the stimuli offered by the environment, and to the development of their creative intelligence.

Simone de Beauvoir describes the feelings of little girls deprived of the opportunities to try physically to conquer difficult objectives. Even though it is a description of little girls more than 20 years ago, it still remains completely valid.

> They are doubly envious of the activities peculiar to the boys: first, because they have a spontaneous desire to display their power over the world, and, second, because they are in protest against their inferior status to which they are condemned. For one thing, they suffer under the rule forbidding them to climb trees and ladders or go on roofs. Adler remarks that the notions of high and low have great importance, the idea of elevation in space implying a spiritual superiority, as may be seen in various heroic myths; to attain a summit, a peak, is to stand out beyond the common world of fact as a sovereign subject (ego); among boys climbing is frequently a basis for challenge. The little girl, to whom such exploits are forbidden and who, seated at the foot of a tree or cliff, sees the triumphant boys high above her, must feel that she is, body and soul, their inferior. And it is the same if she is left *behind* in a race or jumping match, if she is thrown *down* in a scuffle or simply kept on the side lines.[5]

What stops girls from competing against each other or with boys in these games in which physical dexterity plays such a great part? If they had a strong desire to compete they would surely attempt those undertakings which attract them and from which they suffer from being excluded. The fact is that if they gave way to their impulses they would draw attention to the fact that they were behaving in an anomalous way. Children cannot bear to feel different from others of the same age, because any difference will make them be judged as 'strange'. They will be rejected and criticised. Conformity is necessary because they have a need of rules and models to reassure them.

A teacher in a village nursery school told me that a pupil of five was subjected daily to attacks from her six-year-old brother. Since the little girl was tall and strong and therefore perfectly capable of facing up to him and beating him, the teacher suggested to her that she should try and hit back. The girl answered that her mother would not like it because 'he is a boy and only Daddy can touch him'. Not even the mother dared intervene when he became enraged at the little girl. All she would do was to help the girl barricade herself inside her bedroom in order to escape her brother's fury. The child thought it quite natural that things should be so, because her mother was herself beaten by the father and did not react, and she had adhered to such an extent to this particular concept of the female rôle and the social group to which she belonged that she didn't even feel any urge to defend herself from her brother's attacks.

A young woman told me that from childhood she had played almost exclusively with boys of her own age, of whose deeds she was almost always the admiring observer. The boys often showed scorn for her weakness. They would feel her arms so as to prove how worthless girls were because they had no muscles, and she was very humiliated by these episodes. Finally one day, one of the boys provoked her so much that she reacted like a fury, attacking him and fighting him under the very eyes of the group. She managed to beat him by getting him down with his shoulders to the ground. This victory filled her with pride, but it was very short-lived because both the defeated boy and all the others, instead of admiring her for her physical strength as one would have expected, found a way of humiliating her once again by telling her that she was not a girl but a boy, because girls cannot fight boys. This episode struck her profoundly and greatly undermined her confidence. From that moment on her relationship with the group of boys was always dogged by the question of how she should behave. She wanted to be thought of as a girl and so she no longer joined in physical contests with them, but in order to salvage her self-esteem which had been so badly knocked, she needed a way to get her own back, and she found it in verbal aggression. She began

to attack the boys with sarcasm and insults. In this way she developed a way of competing which was no longer based on playing
and fighting, but on intellectual superiority which worked perfectly as she was the most intelligent of the group and her strength
was such that she became the head of it, 'the brain'. It was she who
thought up the games, instigated them and directed them. All the
same, her relationships with boys were problematical and continue
to be so with men.

The lively creative little girl, full of energy, always feels a subtle
sense of unease and guilt if she competes with boys in games of
strength. She obscurely realises that she is not approved of, that
she is disappointing the expectations of others. Continually before
her eyes is the image of the girl she will never succeed in being.
No one will be pleased if she is combative, courageous, loyal and
independent. They would prefer her to be docile, conformist, timid
and hypocritical, even though later on they will criticise her for
being so.

Female development can be defined as permanent frustration.

It is essential that the social personality of each individual should
evolve in such a way as to correspond to his biological sex, so that
the boy should have boys' habits and the girl should have girls'
habits. Sex-typing seeks to prepare children for their future rôles as
parents. This typing, although obviously already established in a
biological sense, develops from the still unformed behaviour of early
infancy. For example, boys learn that they must not fight with their
sisters but must fight with children of their own age and sex if they
don't wish to be called cissies. Girls must learn that nice young
ladies don't climb trees even if boys do; boys have to understand that
it is not manly to play with dolls after a certain age, even if they
did so at first. Boys have to learn that tears are not a proper way of
reacting to a conflict situation, while it is hardly ever insisted that
girls should give up such behaviour. Besides all this, girls have to
learn not to cross their legs when sitting down, while for boys these
precautions are quite unnecessary. And the list could continue
indefinitely, but it is enough to have pointed out those changes in
behavioural development which are imposed in order to effect sex-
typing and which must be considered to a greater or lesser degree as
frustrations. In some cases adults still show a tendency to rebel
against the prohibition of primitive forms of behaviour.[6]

Dollard seems rather hurried in this analysis, which raises
various objections: sex-typing does not seek to prepare children

for their rôles as future parents, but to prepare girls for the rôle of wife and mother and boys for their future as the holders of power. The sex-typing which is already established in a biological sense only relates to procreation. All the rest is cultural unless it can be proved otherwise. From the short list of social rules cited by Dollard it is evident that the balance of frustration resulting from restriction to a required sexual model weighs decisively against girls. What frustration is there for boys in not being allowed to fight with girls, for example, compared to being absolutely forbidden to come to blows at all? If frustration, as Dollard maintains, engenders aggression, girls who are so much more frustrated than boys should develop it to a far greater degree. It probably is true, only here one obstacle is added to another, because free expression of their aggression is also forbidden to them. Their condition would be unbearable if they could not find some other way of expressing it, such as auto-aggression, verbal aggression (insults, spiteful talk, gossip) and even negative psychosomatic reactions such as inhibitions, stereotyped behaviour (in which the realistic and self-restricting games we have examined play a part), anxiety-ridden perfectionism and ambivalence.

But this is not enough. In exchange for their self-control girls are offered compensations which are just as attractive in appearance but which turn out to be real limitations to the realisation of one's potential as an individual: the high value attached to beauty, the excessive attention and care given to one's external appearance, encouragement of narcissism, greater opportunities for displaying one's emotions. There is little authenticity in all this. All girls remain impotent rebels underneath, constrained to calculate at each moment whether it is better to abandon oneself to rebellion or to subject oneself to dependence. Those with more life in them will fight longer and more painfully than others. But the dilemma will persist throughout their lives and confront them at every choice. It will keep them in a perpetual state of disengagement and expectation.

Children's literature

A group of feminists from the city university of Princetown, New Jersey,[7] analysed in one year 15 sets of books for children and 144 reading texts used in elementary schools. Their study reveals that the protagonists in 881 stories are boys, and in only 344 are they girls; that boys go camping, build tree-houses, explore caves, and help daddy, while girls smile, play with dolls and kittens, and cook cakes. The feminists of Princeton sum up in an essay that has just been published that 'from the first years of elementary school our children learn that males are dominating and women passive'. In the 144 reading texts for elementary schools, mothers are seen in the kitchen; in reality 40% of American mothers work in factories and offices.

The feminists of Princeton united with a group of women in New York to edit a national report on the sexual prejudice nourished by children's books. Common to the books was the theme that exciting activities are reserved for boys while girls are deliciously incapable creatures or noble helpers.

Alix Schulman, a writer from New York, shows that the most common figure in children's books is the typical mother who is in the kitchen. In cases where the mother works her occupation is always run-of-the-mill, subordinate, of little value, a job traditionally regarded as feminine: shorthand typist, waitress, nurse, schoolteacher. One book alone has a scientist mother, but her husband is a superscientist and so here too the subordinate relationship is respected.

The feminist committee also examined 1,000 novels for children and produced a proper index of 'forbidden books' which is distributed to libraries, schools, and parent-teacher associations throughout the United States. Out of the 1,000 books examined only 200 were saved and the other 800 were judged as 'irremediably sexist'.

These initiatives had a variety of repercussions at the next reunion of the Association of Authors and Publishers of Children's Books. Some of these defended themselves by explaining that they published more books for boys because girls will not read books for girls. As a result of this work by the American feminists, many editors started work on collections of books dedicated to more or less famous women and books which had female characters as protagonists.

In the French periodical, *L'ecole des parents*, there appeared a paper written by M. J. de Lauwe entitled *The Child and his Image* [8] in which de Lauwe analysed the characters of children and adults as they appear in French books and films for children, and 'the way in which these images are perceived and interpreted by the children for whom they are intended'.

These idealized characters embody the concepts of adults, the proper values of the culture into which the children are being initiated.

Because they are imaginary, they offer the opportunity to escape, thereby compensating for the restrictions imposed by the child's surroundings and by his own personality. As they belong to the same age group, children can easily identify with them. These characters are created by the adults according to their own conception of childhood and their own fantasies in relation to children.

Among the texts examined, those written for boys contain exclusively male characters, while those written for girls contain 57% male characters and 43% female. In the texts intended for both sexes, male characters predominate by far. At the same time, the familiar female characters who generally accompany the hero here grow fewer. There are more fathers and less mothers.

'The uneasiness of society in relation to women is revealed in these stories. Girls find themselves confronted by a representation of the world from which women are almost totally excluded.' The few female characters are almost all on a lower level, making pure and simple appearances of no importance, and only in the capacity of servants. Even when groups of children are represented they have an authoritarian structure and the leader is always a boy, never a girl. A mother–daughter relationship is rare, a mother–son relationship almost unheard of. Next to the protagonists of either sex there often appears an uncle who has an important rôle in the story.

This collection of facts reveals the uncertainty of feminine images in our society and may explain at least in part the difficulty girls have in accepting their sex and in identifying with it. In fact various studies on this subject have shown that many girls would have preferred to be boys, while the opposite is exceptional.

The ambivalence of girls towards their sex is confirmed by their choice of a favourite character: 45% of girls actually choose a male to identify with and admire, while only 15% of boys admire female characters. When, during the enquiry, children of both sexes were asked if they would like to be a certain male character, 95% of the boys said they would and so did a third of the girls. The authors of children's books limit themselves punctiliously to offering children the same models that have already been set up by the family and the social environment. Children's literature, therefore, has the simple function of confirming the models which children have already absorbed. The transmission of cultural values becomes a powerful chorus with no dissenting voice.

An author of dramatic texts for children told me that when he had tried to write a script that had as its protagonist a girl who departed from tradition by being wilful, courageous, a leader, he had had serious difficulties in finding a suitable way of talking and acting for her. The script had emerged as inconsistent, barely credible and difficult to act. To him, this meant that it required a great effort, especially as a man, to forget the social reality in which one is steeped and to introduce new social values. In this case, then, he contented himself with attributing characteristics normally considered male to a female character.

Not only do the writers of children's books not make an effort to promote new values, they actually present models which are inferior to reality.

In the same French journal, *L'ecole des parents*,[9] there was an enquiry by Michèle de Wilde in which French and American female stereotypes were compared. In reference to children's literature, the author states that in the United States a record catalogue of children's books which is used by thousands of teachers gave two lists of titles, one suitable for boys and one suitable for girls. The vocabulary used in conjunction with these titles is rich in implications. Boys 'decipher and discover', 'learn and train themselves', or 'conquer' someone or something. Girls 'struggle', 'overcome difficulties', 'feel at a loss', or 'help to resolve'. Some girls 'learn to face the real world' or 'experience difficulty in adapting'. The texts used for learning to read offer children the image of a typical American family: a mother who does not work, a father who does, two children of whom the older is always a boy, and two animals, dogs or cats, whose age and sex follow the same pattern as the children. In these textbooks the boys build cabins, climb fences and so on, while the girls go shopping, help the mother to cook, play at being grown ladies or with dolls, clean their rooms or help people in distress. The passages describing them often show their inability to do something like skate or ride a pony.

It is a fact that many girls today are extremely good at skating or at riding ponies, but only those who cannot do these things are considered interesting. In spite of the many real examples which counteract these models, the image of girls as fragile and incapable continues to be promulgated. Adults seem to be incapable of abandoning the myth of the eternal female. Completely blind to the new physiognomy of real children which has fortunately changed in the meantime, even if it has not changed as much as it might, writers continue to produce idealised and nostalgic images of an improbable sort of childhood. The extension of this phenomenon operates in such a way that it seems to be programmed. Because of the crystallisation of writers' views, children's books are the least liable to fulfil their potential function of breaking the conventional order of things and proposing new values of greater wealth and variety. Girls who, in spite of being extremely good at sporting activities, see themselves presented by children's books as idealised models of fragility and ineptitude, cannot but feel the discomfort and unease of one who does not know to which model she should conform.

In Italy, too, children's literature and school textbooks are beginning to be analysed and criticised for anachronistic, unhistorical and sexist content. But awareness of this problem is limited to feminist groups and to a few publicists and journalists, while those who are concerned with children's education, including the parents, do not notice it at all.

The daily paper *Il Giorno* [10] published an enquiry into textbooks in use in primary schools here, and on the way which male and female figures are presented therein. The article was cited on the woman's page, which excluded any men from pondering over it, as it is well known that they would think it degrading to read the woman's page. In the textbooks examined, the typical family follows certain patterns; father, mother, and two babies, the elder of whom is always a boy. This does not differ from what was found in the United States. When they are all at home together, the father reads the newspaper with complete indifference towards his wife and children; the mother sits alone, sewing, since she obviously cannot be allowed either to be idle or to read; the boy, equipped with nuts and bolts, constructs or takes apart his Meccano, and the girl, wearing the classic flowered frock, plays with a doll as sad and disconsolate as herself. Or else the mother is looking after the youngest child, in this case a boy, while the girl looks at her in admiration, obviously anxious to imitate. We are not told that very soon this boy will be entrusted to her in the moments when she is free from school and from homework, such is the attention with which she has applied herself to her apprenticeship, feeding and attending to her dolls. There is no mother who goes out to work, or who gives herself the rest she deserves, or amuses herself in some way. If she is portrayed sitting in a chair, one may be certain that she is darning or embroidering, while her daughter, composed and judicious, watches her and learns. If two children are playing, the boy will be stretched out on the floor, his shoes thrown one here and one there, his sleeves rolled up, his cap at a rakish angle on his head, decidedly at his ease among constructional toys, a ball, and a big lorry. The girl does not join in these games. She sits to one side, composed, neat, irreproachable, with the eternal doll in her arms. Evidently she is meditating on her future as a wife and mother. The mother at home does everything for love, with a sweet smile on her lips, which gives one to suppose that it is no trouble to her; so much so that when her man returns home from work and wants to rest in his armchair, she continues without rest. She does it all for nothing. 'She succeeds in doing alone what elsewhere is done at least by several people', a fact which is inwardly valued by the system, though it takes good care not to recognise it openly for she might become conscious of her own exploitation. It even seems right that she be thus exploited because if she is as idiotic as she is shown to be, she certainly would not know how to do anything else. The father is presented in a completely different way. Not only does he provide food for the family, but he is also its moral and intellectual guide. He teaches rare virtues: not to complain, not to weep, to be silent, to scorn pain; and what is in fact nothing more than inhibition and hardness is made out to be noble pride. He always teaches things which will be useful in life, but his lessons are strictly reserved to the males of the house and the girls are excluded. They remain ignorant or have to content themselves with learning from their mother. Instead, they are conceded the privilege of bringing slippers and newspaper to their father when he returns home tired from work.

From an investigation into textbooks in use in primary schools conducted by Marisa Bonazzi [11] there emerges a chilling picture of the prototype of family life which is offered to children. The mother is a silent, untiring, docile figure at the service of her husband and children. Cooperation is non-existent. In one passage, in which the father is described as 'the head of the tribe' (a word which pleases mummy so much), he is seen going to the town hall to make arrangements, buying medicines, paying the grocer's bill. When he does the night shift in the car factory where he is employed, he spends the whole of the subsequent morning shopping in the market. In contrast to this unbridled efficiency are the grandmother who does the ironing and the mother whose activities are nowhere mentioned. The interest of the father is centred on the youngest child, a boy, naturally: 'He watches him for hours, holds him in his arms and hugs him.'

There is a little poem in which the lack of water in a peasant's house is described as if it were something both joyful and poetic. It needs to be fetched from the well, and the wife is unable to linger at the mirror, because she is obviously overcome by exhaustion.

One passage sings the praises of a mother's hands which are 'useful and humble, loving and tireless. They are useful because they do so much work, humble because they never refuse to do any service, tireless because they are always active.' A perfect description of a slave or a medieval peasant.

In textbooks for primary schools, the woman who works outside the house, who enjoys prestige and has responsibilities, is completely unknown. The only sort described is a masochistic mother figure who does everything for love and answers insults with a gentle smile.

Some significant examples

If one embarks on the fruitless search for books that present new figures, be they male or female, in the field of contemporary children's literature one comes up against works which leave one stupefied. A good example of this is provided by two books which were recently produced by a publisher who specialises in psychological, pedagogical and educational texts, and from whom one might have expected a more enlightened choice of reading for children. It is worth analysing them.[12]

In the first of the two books, *My Family*, appear two children, Paolo Doni and Lucia Monti, who will in the end marry and have twins, Sergio and Luisa, who will be the protagonists of the second book, '*I . . .*'. The childhood and adolescence of Paolo are spent in the following manner. He plays with toy cars and with buckets and spades at the seaside, 'he has studied a lot at school', 'he has learnt a trade', 'he makes friends'.

This is how Lucia spends her childhood and adolescence: she eats a banana, plays with her father, plays with dolls and animals; she goes to school, not alone, of course, but 'with her brother and a friend'; a little sister is born and she already 'knows how to look after her', 'she very much enjoys making herself look pretty' (and she is in fact described in front of a mirror intent on making herself up), and 'she goes on outings with her friends'.

How does the meeting between the two come about? 'Paolo knew many girls' (boys are allowed to) but he thought: 'I think the one I like best is Lucia.' No mention is made of her opinion, she is evidently only granted the privilege of being chosen. We are not actually told that Lucia also 'knew many boys' because it is predetermined that she will only know one and that she will marry that one. 'Paolo and Lucia met each other often. Paolo said: "It is Lucia that I prefer, I love her"'; and we hear why he loves her. 'Lucia often smiles, she's good at housework, Lucia has a gentle character.' Girls should know that they will not be loved for being mischievous, exuberant, and passionate, but only if they are sweet nonentities. Lucia, as we have seen, does not seem to have had many problems; she has been chosen and she accepts without questioning. 'Lucia said to herself: I love Paolo very much. Paolo has a good job, Paolo is kind, Paolo understands me.' She too has calculated it all carefully. Apparently passion does not enter much into this story. They get engaged, prepare for marriage, and marry, all according to the best rules. After they are married Paolo goes to work every day, Lucia stays at home, and at this point an opportune asterisk refers one to the foot of the page where the psychologist Hubbard has in his goodness placed a note: 'one can explain, obviously, that quite a few wives work'.

Twins are born, Sergio and Luisa, the protagonists of the book 'I . . .'. Luisa, already quite big, examines her doll to see where babies come from. Sergio probably already thinks that these are matters for women. While Father reads a book to Sergio, Mother teaches Luisa to wash the dishes; thus one is learning while the other remains ignorant.

When it is announced that a new baby will soon be born, each of the two sees his own world imperilled, but in different ways: Luisa is worried about whether her mother will continue to love her, while Sergio wonders whether his father will still have time to read him books.

A little brother is born, and it is obvious that it will be Luisa who holds him in her arms, just as it is obvious that she will offer the guests sweetmeats at the christening party. Sergio, of course, doesn't care and instead offers a biscuit to the dog.

As though this collection of conventional characters and brutally discriminatory situations were not enough, we are presented with Aunt Elena who 'would have liked to marry but could not find a man whom she really liked.' As she is unmarried, no one supposes that she could be a woman with a particularly free and independent profession, but we are told that she is a schoolteacher, a typically feminine profession, and that she has of course plenty of time to devote to others.

The second book, '*I* . . .', offers children a series of reflections on themselves, on their bodies, and on their relationships with others. Sergio and Luisa are always dressed in blue and pink respectively. 'You're the mother,' it says on page two, 'you prepare the meals, you do so many other things (she is laden with shopping bags), you look after me (she is putting the baby to bed), you talk to Daddy.' In the eloquent illustration father is sitting in an armchair, his legs crossed, with slippers, newspapers and pipe, and seems to be giving a benevolent hearing to the mother who is standing in front of him with a timid and provisory air.

'I am a child' is the next concept, and we see the two children playing ball together. But in the following illustration their rôles are deeply divided as the girl says, 'I am drying the dishes', and the boy, sitting at the table with his school books, says, 'I'm studying.' The message is quite clear: girls work, boys study.

'Sergio is a boy,' the next page proclaims, therefore he has a pistol in his hand and other emblems of his sex around him – a ball, a lorry and a bicycle. 'When he is big he will be a man and a man can be a Daddy', and we see the father showing Sergio a bench full of carpenter's tools, a symbol of his future professional life.

'Luisa is a girl' is established on the next page. She has in fact a doll in her hand, and nearby is a little pink dress hanging on a hook, another doll sitting on a set table, and a pair of scales with some cherries. The sum of which is still today taken to represent the condition of girlhood. 'When she is big she will be a woman, and a woman can have babies', and we actually see her pushing a pram with a little girl in it and holding a little boy by the hand. No mention is made of her future profession. Throughout the book, whenever other children appear, the oldest is always a boy.

'In order to grow,' the text continues, 'I need to move, to breathe, to think and to sleep: I also need to learn.' Here we see the boy seated at a table intent on exercising his brain with constructional toys; 'to help in the home' – here is a scene of the girl wearing the apron that is the hallmark of those who serve, collecting the sweepings off the floor with a dustpan and brush. One would deduce from this that the biological process of growth differs totally between the two sexes, given that the male needs to nourish his brain with learning, but the girl needs to remain as ignorant as possible except for learning to sweep.

'In order to grow,' continues the book, 'Sergio and Luisa also need to play', and fortunately this time they both play, but she with the eternal doll while he plays with a lorry; 'to sleep' and here the pink and blue of their clothes is extended to their pyjamas, bedcovers and slippers. Whereas Sergio sleeps with a big coloured ball beside his bed, symbolising his dynamic games, Luisa has instead the doll, which seems to be the only toy which she has at her disposal, together with a teddy bear.

Still in order to grow, 'I need to be loved and to love'. Here the message becomes more subtle. Who must love and who must allow themselves to be loved? The boy goes off on his scooter, very serious, almost surly, the girl, smiling sadly, waves goodbye and watches him go away, because it is obviously she who loves and who stays behind. Throughout the book the boys smile very rarely, but the girls smile all the time.

Besides the need to love, one also needs to 'talk to others' in order to grow; but in this case it is two little boys who are talking to each other. In other words the need to communicate is a masculine need. Women only chatter, and anyway what could a boy and girl have to say to each other given that he reads, studies, plays with a greater variety of things and goes off on his own, while she does not read or study but only plays with her doll, stays at home, and only knows how to dry the dishes?

'To see beautiful things . . .', and here the family is gathered in front of the lighted fire. While the father is sitting down and smoking his pipe, the mother is darning, because she obviously cannot be expected to be sitting down and doing nothing. The parents' attitudes are faithfully reproduced by the two children: the boy is half lying on the floor looking at the fire while the girl fans it. 'To do beautiful things': the boy is painting, the girl is embroidering. 'I need to take pride in what I do': the girl is ironing, the boy is hoeing around the lettuces.

Any activity which is meant to be difficult and to require strength and dexterity, such as trying to shut a box, is only shown as being undertaken by the father and the son. The women are obviously judged incapable.

The series of messages concludes in this way: 'Sometimes I am happy' and we see the boy with a big cake; 'proud' and here is the girl with a pile of carefully folded towels in her arms. 'Sometimes I am sulky' and naturally it is the boy who is sulking, since the girl is always smiling. 'Sometimes I am afraid', and here it is of course the girl who is afraid, according to the convention. 'I am filled with wonder', here it is the boy who is standing entranced in front of a goldfish in a bowl. Evidently girls are not supposed to be capable of experiencing emotions of an intellectual or aesthetic nature.

In the 'First Adventures' series, published by Mondadori, is a book entitled *First Adventures in the World of Words*, by A. Holl, which exudes the same sexism as the above-mentioned texts, if a little more subtly. On page 32 we read: 'On the way home we saw people occupied in various activities; some men putting up scaffolding, children playing, a peasant working in the fields, and a lady out for a walk.' What else do ladies do if not go for walks? Work outside the walls of their home does not seem to exist for them. On page 37 it says: 'You can do many things which animals cannot do. You can dress yourself', and we see a boy dressing. 'You can help Mummy', and inevitably it is a girl who is helping her, but at 'You can paint', it is once more a boy painting. On page 48 it says: 'Words help Mummy in her work', and the mother is depicted in the kitchen consulting a recipe book. But the same words 'Give Daddy the latest news', and there he is reading the paper, so that children learn that women are semi-literate and only interested in reading if it helps them to decipher recipes, while men who have far more interests use words to inform themselves on world events.

In another volume in this series, *First Adventures in the World of Forms and Signs*, by Thoburn and Reit, one page shows a number of boys playing in the park while the girls watch them. One boy has climbed a tree and a girl is watching him from below full of admiration. At the foot of another tree, there is a boy reading who has his own good girl in front of him, watching, and yet another is buying a balloon, and he too has his own astonished girl in tow.

In the next volume, *First Adventures in the World of Reflections*, by Holl, two boys build a tree-house with their father but there is no sign of any girls. On another page the boys gather apples, while the girls, in the best tradition, pick flowers. A boy dreams of becoming a mechanic, a fireman, a pirate, an astronaut, a cowboy, an Indian, and a footballer, but there are no corresponding dreams for girls. It is understood that girls do not have dreams about their future or if they do they are dreams of love, motherhood, or the house they will look after.

The dreams of the future which girls are permitted are illustrated in a book published in the United States.[13] It is worth quoting a bit of the text in order to demonstrate its transparently clear message.

> Whistle Mary whistle
> and you shall have a cow
> I can't whistle mother
> because I don't know how.
> Whistle Mary whistle
> and you shall have a pig
> I can't whistle mother
> because I'm not so big.
> Whistle Mary whistle
> and you shall have a sheep
> I can't whistle mother
> because I'm asleep.
> Whistle Mary whistle
> and you shall have a trout
> I can't whistle mother
> because my tooth is out.
> Whistle Mary whistle
> and you shall have a goat
> I can't whistle mother
> because it hurts my throat.
> Whistle Mary whistle
> and you shall have a pie
> I can't whistle mother
> because my mouth is dry.
> Whistle Mary whistle
> and you shall have the moon
> I can't whistle mother
> because I've lost the moon.
> Whistle Mary whistle

> and you shall have a man –
> tweet, tweet, tweet,
> I just found out I can!

The goals towards which girls like Mary should strive are defined. They are not the pleasures of the world, symbolised by animals, sweets and the moon. Girls should reserve their energies for something really worthwhile, that is, getting themselves a man. There is not much difference between Mary who refuses to whistle and the various Sleeping Beauties, Snow Whites and Cinderellas. Fashions change, somewhat quite considerably, but female figures are always passive and inept, without ambitions or ideals apart from capturing a man who will make them 'live happily ever after!'

When in children's literature a woman is presented who is not completely passive and inept, her character is distorted to the point of making her into a witch. A case in point in 'Pulcinella's Tarantella',[14] which is a Neapolitan version of the well-known fairy tale about the goldfish. It is a decidedly misogynous story in which Pulcinella, together with his wife, five children and a cat 'lived in a hovel without a door and without a roof, and his bed was made of straw and in that bed slept eight: five children, the wife, and the cat.' But in spite of this dramatic poverty, Pulcinella contents himself with fishing, and what is more, with little results. Nonetheless he maintains his extremely good humour: 'It is already three days since we have eaten – and my husband has started to dance.' Amid this demented gaiety, 'only the wife is full of rage, she seems like a wild beast in a cage'.

Pulcinella, goaded by his wife, returns to his fishing and finds the goldfish, which in return for liberty promises to fulfil his every desire. Pulcinella is not even capable of using this opportunity to resolve his family's plight. He contents himself with asking for a certain amount of spaghetti, not being able to see beyond the end of his nose. The family satisfy their hunger and when they are finally full, they all sing in chorus: except for the wife who says, 'Fine, sing, but who is thinking of tomorrow?' She is justly preoccupied and anguished by their chronic poverty and by the burden of five children and an irresponsible husband. It is she who asks the fish through Pulcinella for a real house with at least seven beds. They are all happy to be sleeping at last each in his own bed, but who could resist the temptation to ask the magic fish for as much as possible? The poor wife, made wicked by her past sufferings, and determined to have all the things she has never had all at once, knows no limits. She demands two maids, a baroque drawing room, a radio, a television, a villa at the seaside, a fur coat for herself and clothes for the children. As this progress towards riches continues, she does truly exaggerate and makes the absurd request for a queen's crown for herself and a throne for Pulcinella. In a final fit of folly the wife asks for the goldfish cooked and seasoned, and then everything disappears and the family find themselves back in their hovel.

Ugo d'Ascia,[15] on the subject of the negative characters in fairy tales, acutely remarks: 'Behind the "wicked" stepmothers, witches and ogresses in which fairy tales abound, there is always a weak man who is unloading all the most thankless tasks and decisions on to her.'

Old tales

If one compares the female figures of contemporary children's literature with those of the traditional fairy tales, one realises that little has changed. The old fairy tales contain meek, passive, inarticulate women who are concerned only with their own beauty and are quite inept and useless. On the other hand the male figures are active, strong, courageous, loyal and intelligent. Nowadays fairy tales are hardly ever told to children. Television and stories invented for them have provided a substitute. But some of the most famous tales have survived and everybody knows them.

'Little Red Riding Hood' is the story of a girl, bordering on mental deficiency, who is sent out by an irresponsible mother through dark wolf-infested woods to take a little basket full to the brim with cakes, to her sick grandmother. Given these circumstances her end is hardly surprising. But such foolishness, which would never have been attributed to a male, depends on the assurance that one will always find at the right moment and in the right place a brave huntsman ready to save grandmother and granddaughter from the wolf.

Snow White is also a silly little goose who accepts the apple she is offered, although she has been severely warned not to trust anybody. When the seven dwarfs accept her as a guest, the rôles reappear. They go off to work while she keeps their house clean, mends their clothes, sweeps and cooks and waits for their return. She too lives with her head in the clouds. The only quality she is recognised as having is beauty. Since beauty is a natural gift, which is not affected by the will of the individual, this does her very little credit. She always manages to get into trouble, and in order to get her out of it a man must, as usual, intervene: Prince Charming, who will marry her according to rule.

Cinderella is the prototype of domestic virtues: humility, patience, servility and 'under-developed consciousness',[16] and she is not very different from the female types described in everyday textbooks for primary schools and in children's literature. She too does not move a finger to get out of an intolerable situation, swallows humiliation and oppression and has neither dignity nor courage. She also accepts being rescued by a man as her only resource, though who can say whether this latter will treat her any better than she has been treated up till then.

'The Ass Skin' competes in submission with Cinderella. Griselda the shepherdess, betrothed to a prince who has found in her the ideal woman, submits to being sadistically oppressed by him because it is one of the exalted female virtues to undergo any amount of bad treatment without rebelling. This feminine ideal has survived in textbooks for children to the extent that the mother is still described as a melancholy and servile creature who always smiles even when she is insulted.

Female figures in fairy tales belong to two fundamentally different categories: the good, but useless, and the wicked. 'It has been calculated that in Grimm's fairy tales 80% of the negative characters are female.'[17]

However diligently one searches, it is impossible to find a female character who is intelligent, courageous, active and loyal. Even the good fairies do not use their own resources, but a magic power which has been conferred on them and which does good with no more logic than does evil in witches. A female character with humane, altruistic motivations, who chooses lucidly and courageously how she will act, is totally non-existent.

The emotional force with which children identify with these characters gives them great powers of suggestion, which are reinforced by innumerable concurring social messages. If it were a case of isolated myths which had survived in a culture which no longer accepted them, their influence could be ignored, but in fact our culture is saturated with the same values that these stories propagate, even if they are somewhat diluted and obscured.

Although this is far from being a comprehensive analysis of

children's literature – which would require another volume – the few examples reported here are significant. They allow one to verify the existence of strong pressures in the area of literature for girls to continue to identify with inferior models of 'femininity'.

The conclusions drawn cannot do other than support the feminists of Princeton and the French researchers. The few texts examined are enough on their own to incriminate children's literature, which is responsible for a discriminatory, reactionary, misogynist and anti-historical dialectic. This is all the more serious when one is aware that such distortions are passed on to children who accept them without being able to criticise them. The models proposed by this type of literature rather than helping the child to develop and to organise his future society, risk stunting him in infancy. Such representations of childhood are not without consequences for adults, parents and educators, who instead of being encouraged to imagine a new type of child, a new relationship with him and the new position which he will occupy in society, are forced back into the old models which should have been definitively abandoned. In this respect children's literature fails completely in its function.

Notes

1 Jean Chateau, *Il gioco del fanciullo*, in Maurice Debesse, op. cit., p. 222.
2 Charles Bried, *Gli scolari e le scolare*, in Maurice Debesse, op. cit., p. 346.
3 Erik Erikson, *Childhood and Society*, Penguin Books, London 1965.
4 Charles Bried, op. cit., p. 346.
5 Simone de Beauvoir, *The Second Sex*, Penguin Books, London 1972, pp. 313–314.
6 John Dollard, *Frustration and Aggression*, Yale University Press, London 1939.
7 *Panorama* (an Italian periodical), 28 October 1971.
8 *L'ecole des parents*, no. 3, March 1972.
9 Michelle de Wilde, 'Les sterotypes feminins', in *L'ecole des Parents*, no. 7, July–August 1972.
10 Lorenza Zanuso, 'Cenerentole per forza', in *Il Giorno*, 18 February, 1972.
11 Marisa Bonazzi and Umberto Eco, *I pampini bugiardi*, Guaraldi, Florence 1972. For further analysis of children's literature see Egidia Barassi and Stefano Magistretti, *Il leggere inutile*, Emme,

Milan 1972 and Alberti, Bini, del Corno and Rotondi, *I libri di testo*, Editori Riuniti, Rome 1972. In English, see *Racist and Sexist Images in Children's Literature*, Paper 1 and Paper 2, especially the article *Presentation of Sex Rôles in British Reading Schemes*, Glenys Lobban, Writers and Readers Publishing Cooperative 1975; *Children's Books, A Statement and Lists*, Children's Rights Workshop, London 1974.

12 Denise Roques, *La mia familia*, Armadon, Rome 1971; Denise Roques and Odile Julien, *Io . . .*, Armando, Rome 1971.

13 *Whistle Mary Whistle*, adapted by Bill Martin Jr., with pictures by Emanuele Luzzati, Holt, Rinehart and Winston, New York 1970.

14 Emanuele Luzzati, *La tarantella di Pulcinella*, Emme, Milan 1972.

15 Ugo d'Ascia, 'Onorevolmente cattive' in *Noi donne*, no. 50, 19 December 1971.

16 Enzo Rava, 'Se il principe non le avesse baciate?' in *Noi donne*, no. 50, 19 December 1971.

17 Ugo d'Ascia, op. cit.

CHAPTER IV

EDUCATIONAL INSTITUTIONS: NURSERY, PRIMARY AND SECONDARY SCHOOLS

> 'I have a willy to make a wee
> and a place to make a pooh.
> You have a place to make a pooh
> and another which is good for nothing.'
> *Refrain sung by a little boy of six
> to a little girl of the same age.*

Schools for children from the age of three to six are called nursery schools. The old expression 'nursery' school was not exhumed from tradition by chance, but after mature reflection by those who recast law 444 of 18 March 1968 and instituted a new state school for pre-scholars.* The term 'nursery' school – which was preferred to the 'infant school' suggested by psychological–pedagogical researchers – implies a condensed hodge-podge of ideas about childhood. These ideas seem to be at once obtuse, conjectural, scientific and melodramatic. They bring together a falsely sugary view of motherhood with an equally false, sentimental and affected view of the child. The child continues to be seen as an innocent little idiot, perpetually astonished and stupefied by what goes on around him. 'He's little, he doesn't understand anything, anyhow.' A spectator in life, he will not be permitted to become an active protagonist until he reaches adulthood.

But the child *is* a person to be taken seriously.

He is a remarkable worker – persistent, untiring, attentive, lucid and precise. From the moment he comes into the world, he is a courageous, insatiable and curious explorer, who makes use of his senses and intelligence much in the same way as a scientist. All his energies are given over to the search for knowledge. He tries and tries again, fails and begins all over with an infinite patience, until he has attained what he considers to be perfection. He is always ready to take chances, to expose himself to derision in an adult world made for adults. Rather than favouring him, this adult world shackles him and makes him the butt of laughter, commisera-

* This refers to the Italian system.

tion, a protective paternalism or simply indifference. Meanwhile the child carries on, always on the verge of discouragement or total failure, always aware of his own weakness and impotence, always attempting to come to grips with people, objects and situations which for him are difficult or even crushing.

The young child has the instincts of a vagabond who is curious about everything and wants to experience everything within the moment. He is strongly attracted by other people and confronts them without adult dissimulation, detours or compromises. His peers provide an irresistible attraction. To spend time with them, he is ready to undergo all risks and dangers, suffer violent rejections, cruel blows and the toughest battles. His conquests may be precarious, rather than definitive; but that does not seem to matter. He is always ready to start all over again, bravely exposing himself to poor treatment, physical confrontation, bites and scratches with a courage which only belongs to those of his own age, and *which is identical in both sexes*. No adult would be ready to do or suffer so much merely to establish and maintain social contact. But the child is prepared for anything.

Someone who is so brave and lives with such intensity deserves not only to be autonomous, but to be unconditionally encouraged, approved and admired. He should be given the means and tools necessary for his explorations. As one does for a researcher one should respect him and leave him in peace. Equally he should be given the strength to free himself from the family and its emotional ties so that he can open himself to broader social relations. Instead of this the child remains at the mercy of his parents, whose sole fear is that he will detach himself from them.

In fact, as soon as the child does begin to free himself from familial ties and especially from his natural mother – an enterprise which is extremely painful because she restrains and discourages him and makes him feel guilty – he is given another mother. This second mother bears less of an emotional link to him, but she is just as little prepared to understand what a surprisingly ingenious and enterprising little worker she has to deal with. Just as the mother above all the dispenser of love – and her manner of loving, even when she commits gross errors, is by definition the right one, since it is dictated by her biological ties with her child – nursery school teachers are conceived of as the perpetrators of this task of loving.

This is where the rhetoric of so called mother-love triumphs. If it were subjected to a clear, lucid analysis, this mother-love would be revealed as a repressive tool, based on blackmail, paralysing to the child. Yet even if this type of love were beneficial to very young children, it could still be superfluous and anachronistic to make of it the model of 'ideal' relations between nursery school teachers and their pupils. By the age of three, if not earlier, the child needs culture rather than stifling emotional ties.

The only person who is deemed capable of caring for children of this age, is a woman. Precisely because she is a woman, it is assumed that she has the natural talents of gentleness, patience, understanding and calm. It is thought, too, that her situation as an actual or potential mother must 'instinctively' suggest to her what behaviour is best suited to each and every circumstance. But are we certain that these qualities are precisely the ones which permit this extraordinary explorer – which the child of three is – to master the world and make it his own? Are we sure that these talents can stimulate his development and will not rather serve to hold him back for a longer time than necessary in his dependent and power-less position? Who in fact are these teachers to whom the law entrusts children just at the moment when they should be living most intensely? This is, after all, an age which should be one of the most fecund and creative. Any educative intervention at this stage in a child's development is destined to leave an almost in-eradicable mark.*

The 'career' of a nursery school teacher often appeals to young women who are totally devoid of ambition, independence and a desire for self-realisation. First of all the study period is extremely brief and the intellectual preparation needed is minimal. Then the widespread prejudice which states that if one is a woman, one has a particular aptitude for taking care of children, especially very small ones, encourages young women to choose a profession on the sole basis of self-interest.

For young women of the working class and petty bourgeoisie, to be a schoolteacher still represents an important social promo-tion: in effect, except in rare cases, young women from the upper social strata refrain from entering the teaching profession since to them it seems quite devoid of attraction.

Nursery school teaching is seen as a part-time occupation with

* We have omitted here a section pertaining to the training of Italian schoolteachers since this does not approximate to the British situation.

a salary which, for a woman, is fair for the number of hours put in. There are a good many holidays during the year and an extended summer vacation. And the pay is regular for those who are not supply teaching. Choosing the profession for such reasons – which though not unworthy are hardly noble – is really rather dangerous. An essential feature is being totally disregarded: nursery school teaching is not just any profession, but an activity which leaves an indelible imprint on children of three. Few of our teachers seriously ask themselves if they are cut out for this kind of work. Most people are still convinced – as if we continued to live in a time when psychological factors were totally unheard of – that anyone can deal with children. And since at the age of three children are illiterate, it is thought quite natural for the person who takes care of them to be so too.

The question of a teacher's quality is considered, but only where knowledge is concerned and as a function of the age of the students. In secondary school or university, the young are in contact with teachers of a superior kind. These, however, are much more necessary in the early years of childhood when a lack of consciousness and the critical faculty which stems from it, makes the child infinitely more vulnerable than he is later on.

The social and economic reasons for choosing the profession of nursery school teacher are those we have looked at. But if teachers are questioned, they rarely admit to such motivation – either because they are unaware of it or because they know that it is not permissible to admit to such materialistic intent in professions of this kind. In fact, most teachers claim to have a 'vocation'. The term 'vocation' has undertones of a near mystical calling. It implies a desire to make oneself socially useful, an almost total disinterest for the economic side of the activity, an altruism, and especially a spirit of self-sacrifice. Curiously enough, the term is only used for those professions which concern themselves with the human being in aspects generally thought of as degrading; childhood, old age, physical and mental illness, abnormality, etc. Self-sacrifice is always suspect. It is hard to imagine what motives might bring a healthy person spontaneously to sacrifice himself rather than enjoy life. And self-sacrifice in this case entails not only selected moments of existence, but a daily routine for long years without rest.

When a teacher chooses the profession with this kind of self-mortification in view, it would be far better to tell her right at the start that such a motive automatically makes her unsuited to the work. Professions should be chosen because they appeal to us, make us happy, enrich and stimulate us – even if occasionally they give rise to momentary situations in which the 'spirit of self-sacrifice' is needed. Children are agreeable and attractive.

The very nature of their physical persons can seduce and move the adult to take care of them, as Eibl-Eibesfelt says.[1] Children should evoke the adult's tenderness, please and amuse him, awaken in him positive feelings of empathy, interest and curiosity, which make him feel he is on their side and identifies with them. If the adult has to call the educative relationship a 'vocation', it is because he does not particularly like children, or at least not enough and not in the way he should. There is nothing wrong with an adult finding children irksome or even antipathetic. This is a psychological question like any other. But in such cases, it is preferable that he is not professionally involved with them. There are many far less dangerous occupations the adult can choose.

I would go even further and say that the use of the term 'vocation' to qualify the teaching profession is inversely proportional to the cultural, professional, and human level of teachers themselves. Among the ones I have observed at work and spoken to, it was precisely those who had good relations with children who professed simply to like their work because they liked children. In no way did they try to present their work as some kind of life-mission. Those, on the contrary, who felt children to be tedious and insufferable found it necessary in one form or another to attach the slogan 'vocation' to their work.

The psychological motives for which an individual chooses to be a teacher need to be examined in depth. Often one finds among potential teachers, individuals who have trouble establishing solid and lasting relationships with adults and who are looking for less challenging and frustrating substitutes. In fact, many psychologically disturbed people, with emotional, social and professional problems, ask quite artlessly to be permitted to work with children because, they declare, they have a need to 'give'. They are quite unaware that what they really want in saying this, is to take.

Relationship with an adult demands that one takes the other person into consideration; adapt and come to terms with him. It necessitates an open manifestation of one's demands which, precisely because they may be excessive, inhibited or indirect, are often repulsed or disappointed. But in relationships with children, it is the adult who *leads* – at least in the usual structure of the adult-child relation. The adult's perception of the child as a being dependent on his judgment and approbation leads him to set up an authoritarian and unilateral relation in which he feels he has the dominant rôle without expending any excessive effort. Success is guaranteed. The child will attach himself to such an adult and depend on him, but at what cost, no one can ever say. To derive power – when this is lacking – from a relationship with someone weaker than oneself, is never positive. When the weaker person is a child, this can even become hazardous.

The teacher who consciously or unconsciously chooses her profession as a refuge will inevitably pour all her emotional energy into her work since there is often no other outlet for it. This might be seen as an ideal situation. However, what is in effect happening is that she is bringing an energy into her work which has nothing to do with the pedagogic relationship and which would be better spent elsewhere. If she cannot deploy this energy elsewhere, it is probably because she is inhibited and repressed; and inhibition, like repression, is incompatible with the task of caring for children.

A teacher should not be someone who lives on the fringes of life, but rather a person who has lived and continues to live fully. She should feel herself to be sufficiently fulfilled, not a failure. She should like her equals and not view them with hostility or rancour. For most children, the teacher is the first adult model – outside of parents – they can imitate and identify with. Thus, it is essential that this model be a positive one.

It is evident that nursery school teachers should be able to understand themselves and their behaviour vis à vis their young pupils. This is what teacher training colleges ought to prepare them for. Anxieties, defences, reactions to frustration, the reasons for choosing one or another profession, jealousies, likes, aggression, sometimes even sadism have to be analysed and clarified so that the relationships of teachers to children are as clear as possible. Even with consciousness of these areas, the influence of personal problems and the deviation produced by the very nature of existent teaching methods will still remain.

Pedagogical practice is presently undergoing slow and minimal change. There is no lack of new techniques being elaborated and proposed. But the educator – parent or teacher – finds great difficulty in liberating himself from his past and tends to repeat the modalities and attitudes of his own education. It is thus less important for him to learn *how* to treat a child than to embark on self-analysis and see in depth his own past educational experiences and behaviour – for these constitute the fundamental attitudes he holds towards himself and life in general.

Why not men?

If it is true that women, like men, have had a repressive and authoritarian education and that as educators they reproduce received values, it is certain that the weight of this kind of early education bears down more heavily on women.

Men partake of much greater freedom and receive more social consideration than women. Thus they exhibit fewer of the faults which plague people who have had a repressive formation. Why not then propose that men too should act as the educators of children? Why not permit them to teach at nursery school level?

The 'maternal' instinct is wrongly attributed to all women and it serves as the sole basis for their acting as the educators of small children. Yet the existence of a paternal instinct is wholly negated. According to prejudice, the man is not 'naturally' inclined to paternity. It is only slowly and with effort that some – not all – men acquire this form of sensibility and this only when, almost despite themselves, they find themselves to be fathers of already fully formed children. These children, cultural prejudice would have it, remain strange and incomprehensible to the father until such a time when they can express themselves in a fashion akin to his. Only then is the possibility open to him of communicating with them. Thus it is only already mature children who make of each man a father.

Because of his supposedly 'strong nature', the man is not thought capable of experiencing tenderness, a desire to protect, or even an interest in the children he has created as well as children in general. The rôle imparted to him is that of 'provider' of material needs. It is certainly a result of conditioning – quite opposite to that of the woman's – that fatherhood is never presented to a boy as an important event in his life. It is seen, rather, as a secondary and contingent fact and an altogether boring one. The education of children, then, is the woman's affair.

Granted that there are men and women totally unsuited to paternity and maternity, just as there are men and women quite incapable of taking on the rôle of teacher at whatever level. But it would be a mistake to exclude the possibility of there being men who are perfectly suited to the profession of teaching small children. Indeed, because of social prejudice, certain men, endowed with all the characteristics required of education of the very young, do not even think of entering the profession.

Since social and cultural habits, not to mention tradition, wield a heavy weight, the social 'value' of a given profession pays a large part in the adolescent's choice of a future rôle. As far as teaching is concerned, the young boy has to contend with fear of ridicule (It's 'woman's work'); fear of having his virility questioned and of finding himself isolated in a homogeneous group composed of the opposite sex. (Women who enter a masculine profession may be the objects of a sceptical curiosity, but their prestige is increased. Men, on the other hand, who do 'women's work' only evoke derision and commiseration because their status has diminished.)

The youth who goes into teaching on a nursery or primary school level risks being taken for an eccentric, or being considered quite abnormal. The need for justification which is always necessary in such cases reveals how the social compensation available in teaching is judged insufficient for men. Nevertheless history shows us that whenever certain women's professions – such as, for example, obstetrics – have been re-evaluated, whatever the reasons, men have seen some possibility of deriving considerable profit from the change. And as if by anticipation, before appropriating such professions they have ensured that the work's social prestige is augmented.

Presently, certain overtures are being made to introduce men into nursery school teaching. The fact that pedagogues and psychologists have only declared themselves in favour of this has already gone some way towards conferring prestige on the profession. Once enough men are interested in the profession, then the next step, that of bettering financial remuneration, will be taken.

The *Parents Journal* for March April 1972 states that, two male primary school teachers (in the via Ancona and Pestalozzi Schools) were officially posted to afternoon classes for 3 to 6 year olds. Both had passed the final examination qualifying them as registered or supply teachers.

We believe that for the first time in Italy male teachers have made their official entry into Infant School (the Scuola dell Infanza) and thus broken with their secular exclusion from young children's educational institutions. This exclusion, has nothing natural about it and yet most people today still support it for reasons which bear absolutely no relationship either to a correct evaluation of children's psychological needs or a correct pedagogical policy.

Two months after the beginning of their experience, the male teachers declared that they estimated it as a highly positive experiment:

> We can now say that it is necessary seriously to confront all the problems linked with initiating a male teaching presence into children's earliest education. We do not offer this as an alternative to female teachers but as a just complement which is made essential by the very life of the child and by the nature of society. The male presence must not be neglected since it is necessary both for the preparation and the motivation of the child in an educational environment.

Employing two male teachers on afternoons only does not of course offer a full solution to the problem. It would be far better for the men to work full-time and take on the same tasks as female teachers. Otherwise rôle differentiation between the sexes is once again engaged in to the deteriment both of teachers and especially of the children. The latter are forced to draw the perennial conclusion from this situation: that men are supposed to fulfil certain duties and women, others; and in this division of labour, the more worthy and prestigious tasks are reserved for men and the less important ones for women.

During a study day devoted to the psychological problems of teachers (Perouse, 22 May 1968) Giacono Santucci entered into an argument with a parliamentarian who during the debate on state nursery schools had opposed the introduction of male teachers in these terms: 'I don't know how a man could wipe a child's behind!' Santucci pointed out that he was confusing the assistant's duties with the teacher's. Teachers' activities did not include duties which might devalue or declass his person or function.

Apart from these continual and fastidious harpings on notions of prestige, class and value when men are concerned, it is not at all clear that to wipe a child's behind is such as unimportant task that it must be relegated to a secondary person – which is what the assistant is considered to be in relation to the teacher. Everything that happens to a child, everything he experiences has a comparable significance – whether it concerns the heightened spheres of culture and creation or a purely biological phenomenon like dirtying his pants. It would seem to us that the psychological sciences had clearly demonstrated to what an intimate degree the psyche and the body are linked. Nothing which happens to the body can be considered as purely physical; nothing which happens to the mind can be considered as purely psychic. Such apparently crass and banal realities as nutrition and defecation play a psychological rôle and have a strong emotive resonance and a profound fundamental influence on the child's psychic development.

Some of the most important episodes in a child's life take place in toilets. This is especially true when the toilet is not a strictly private place, made use of solitarily and in the most rigorous intimacy. Toilets, especially in nursery schools, should be places where groups of children of both sexes can retire to when they feel like it, and not according to a fixed schedule, since each person has his own and cannot alter it without suffering physically. This is, of course, an ideal, much more comfortable and pleasant than most existent nursery school toilets. It is here that children experience or should experience their first major discoveries about the difference between the sexes. These discoveries give birth to initial questions which should be responded to by those in the group prepared to give them an initial response. It is precisely in the toilet environment that intimate social relations, charged with emotion, are established and consolidated; that personal dialogues take place; that exceedingly delicate situations are sketched and hidden problems emerge. And if an adult were needed here, it should be – of the two teachers assigned to each class – the one who is best prepared psychologically, the one who can best guide certain tensions and conflicts and intervene in order to explain and defuse them.

When will it finally be understood that it is the adult's attitude towards what the child 'produces' which constitutes one of the most formidable and destructive weapons of sexual repression at this age? Very often, as we have seen, the three-year-old has already suffered innumerable painful repressive measures at home. The destructive impact of these ought to be corrected by the one person who should have it in his potential to do so: the teacher.

In the ideal situation, where there is both a male and a female teacher in the classroom, it is essential that a given task is not only performed by one of the two so that a rigid separation of labour ensues. An interchangeability of rôles is indispensable, as is an adaptability to the circumstances and events of the day. This does not negate the fact that certain children will prefer contact either with the male or the female teacher. This choice expresses needs which may not be able to manifest themselves elsewhere, and the teachers must be able to respond to these. The little boy or girl who knows, for example, that he or she can ask to be washed and even changed by the male teacher will ask this of him if it is important to him and satisfies desires he may have of entering into a profound affective relationship with a male figure. Nevertheless when the man and woman have the *same* work to do, it is important that they avoid establishing an automatic hierarchy in which the woman undertakes to do those tasks which, whether rightly or wrongly, are thought to be less difficult or simply 'feminine', and leaves the more prestigious work to the man – who expects such a situation and accepts it quite naturally.

If sex stereotypes are to be destroyed, it is just as well that the work begin early. Children, who, as we have seen, have already assimilated sex stereotypes within the home and seen the supremacy of the male, will find this state of affairs confirmed at school. We could admit that changing a child's dirty nappies is not the most pleasant of tasks – though personally I don't feel this – but if it is pleasant for no one, it is not any more so for a female teacher.

An experiment using male and female teachers in a nursery school classroom was carried out in France. The principal of the school, Lazarine Bergéret, reports on it in the article 'A man in the nursery' ('Un homme a la maternelle') in the journal *L'Ecole des Parents*, November 1971. The article is a vivid document of a study-cycle spent in a nursery school by three young 'social assistants' who were looking for a personal orientation before embarking on specialisation within their profession. The three young men each stayed at the school for a period of two months. They were enthusiastically welcomed by the children who ranged in age from two to six.

The school's regular teacher had previously noted – and whoever has had any contact with nursery and primary schools can confirm this – 'the particular interest which the presence, for whatever reasons, of men in the school elicits from children'.

Delivery men bringing parcels; postmen carrying letters; gardeners who come to prune trees; glaziers replacing broken windows; plumbers repairing taps and toilets; locksmiths fixing locks or soldering reed instruments; electricians climbing on ladders up to the ceiling; sales representatives and 'the cinema man' or 'projectionist' – all attract special attention from the children. 'The knife-grinder, the glazier, the cobbler were invited to execute their work in front of the children, just like musicians, violincellists, flautists and others.'

'For the children in our school, the men who came can only belong to two categories: either they perform some kind of work or they are fathers.'

The young social assistants, however, did do specific work. Rather they simply took care of the children. This did not fail to surprise them and it pleased them greatly. The narrative of this event [2] illustrates better than any commentary can the profound and beneficial influence which the presence of men could have on a community of young children.

> The mere presence of a man in our team seemed to invite, indeed to favour small breakthroughs in numerous children. We couldn't help dreaming what these might have been like if this man had been a qualified teacher informed about and trained for this work.

> From the very first day, from the very first recess, we noted that the children who solicited his attention repeatedly and under thousands of pretexts (toy to repair, a stubborn shoe-lace to tie, game techniques to be bettered), were almost uniquely children without a father, a grandfather or close male relative. These children, sons and daughters of widowed or unwed mothers, of divorced couples or couples with absentee fathers, did not leave the man. The smallest followed him in silence; the braver one touched him and tugged at his trousers or jacket. Within a short time, as soon as he sat down, they would clamber on to his lap – at first using a pretext, but very soon with no second thoughts whatsoever. They seemed to have a real need of forming a lasting relationship with him and of his approbation, which was most often silent. Did the young man's calm and patience really dry tears caused by wounds and arguments, more quickly or were we simply under the illusion that he was more reassuring than we were? Did we merely invert the fact that the bigger boys had grown gentler towards the little ones once they had noted this big man's solicitude towards them?

I myself had a very different but equally conclusive experience in a crèche for children of under two: the arrival of any man, be it a worker who had come to perform some task or simply a visitor, was greeted by manifestations of great joy. Children of both sexes all tugged at his legs demanding that he pick them up. A little girl of two, who had no father, ran gleefully up to everyone and announced, 'There's a man, there's a man!' When a young male friend of one of the teachers came to visit on the very day when the children were to go to the zoo – something they appreciated beyond anything else – they refused to leave the classroom before the young man himself had gone.

Because of their insufficient training and especially because of their personal psychology, nursery school teachers reproduce for children of both sexes a model which is none other than that of their mother. This model is an old, devalued, and troubling one which places obstacles in the path of the children's autonomous development. By the age of three, children are satiated with maternal contact and eager for new experiences. The image of a man who *stays* with them, and fully with them, appeases their perpetually unsatisfied need of being with their father, who is always away or taken up with other interests. The fact that a man – who in their eyes is a fascinating and prestigious being – is finally paying them consistent attention, stimulates them, fills them with pride, heightens their self-esteem and this serves to give them a balance. For little girls the presence of a man who has been trained to be a teacher has an even greater importance. Given the disappointing relationship which little girls have with their fathers – a relationship which excludes them from the male world and offers them in its place a restrictive and frustrating rôle – a masculine presence in the nursery school context could be both highly stimulating and could liberate many energies previously unexpressed.

L. Bergéret writes:

> Should our school in which we rarely worry about 'nursing' perpetually be called a 'nursery school'? Is it necessary to invent a 'paternal' school which stresses the masculine rôle? Wouldn't there be something to strive for in attemping to balance male and female rôles by permitting men to teach in our schools.

The presence of the three 'social assistants' in this nursery school was not only useful to the children and teachers. These young men

> expressed what they called their 'luck' in having been able to share in the professional life of young women. This was especially the case with the last of the three who had been brought up by grandparents. The young men said they had learned to understand our exciting but exhausting profession, and confessed to coming home at night overcome by fatigue. They recognised that they had discovered the problems working women face and had reconsidered their own attitude towards the family in this light.

This statement shows that if one liberates oneself from prejudices, the beneficial consequences can be unexpected, and unforeseen. They can extend so far as to make one analyse and see in a new light much of one's behaviour, which only *apparently* has nothing to do with what provoked it in the first place.

The account of the experience in Bergéret's school invites us to reflect on another point when she states that:

> the children hardly have the opportunity of observing women at work except for those whose work it is to be at their service: teacher, school social worker, service personnel or shopkeepers who are also at one's service and who, in the children's eyes, perform no task but that of cashing money. Why was I, a woman, only tempted to present masculine professions to the children? Is it purely by chance?

Then Bergéret decides that just as they have invited various artisans and professional men to the school, they will now invite women with a profession.

It is not by chance that the principal of the school, an intelligent and open-minded woman, only introduced male workers to these children of two to six. She too is conditioned by stereotyped rôles. She too is intimately persuaded, as all women are, that male work is work, par excellence, while female work is only of secondary importance. It is inevitable that she transmits this prejudice to the children. Only when she is considering something else, does she stumble over this problem and decide to resolve it. But the children have already grasped the situation long before. With their peculiar ability for seeing into the real essence of situations (that is what adults believe is real without necessarily being conscious of it), they have noted that work with a capital W – that on which their survival depends – belongs in the masculine domain. Woman or so it seems to them does not accomplish any authentically productive work, but only takes care of them.

In most cases, the father sees his authority and his relationships with his children reduced simply to his financial contribution. In order to preserve his self-esteem and remain faithful to his rôle as head and supporter of the family, he demands that his work, with the possibility of comfort which it guarantees, be continually present.

Men, too, pay dearly to maintain themselves in the rôle, but they are incapable of renouncing it.

According to the traditional rôle structure, men assume the entire responsibility of supporting their family. They are deprived of all emotional contact with their children and are crushed by responsibilities which often drive them to suffer serious psychic and psychological problems.[3]

This reality is so well understood by children, even when very young, that they will rarely fuss over their father leaving to 'go to the office', but will protest loudly if their mother goes out. They are convinced that the father's rôle is to go to work. The mother, on the other hand, often experiences her work with a strong degree of guilt: to work is to subtract time, energy and affection from her family. To the protests of a small child who she leaves at home or at a crèche, she rarely answers with tranquillity and firmness, 'I have to go to work.' Rather, she reacts with anxiety to her child's demands, which seem to her to be justified since everyone constantly tells her that the child needs her presence in order to develop in a balanced fashion (even though he needs the father's presence just as much).

In the nursery school, little boys and girls find a complete confirmation of the social situation and of the division of male and female rôles. Here, where they are taken care of, men are totally absent. The mother's work, like that of teachers, is not seen as work, properly speaking, but as a service which can be more or less authoritarian, more or less benevolent, but remains nonetheless free. This identification between school teachers and mothers is made to the detriment of little girls. They are forced to identify with the teacher. In the same situation, little boys are convinced that women are contemptible, since they do nothing prestigious, but take care of them. Things are quite different for men. Their mysterious and fascinating work outside the home brings wellbeing to the family and confers upon them both prestige and consideration within the family as well as within the social group to which they belong.

The presence of men in a nursery school setting would give children a realistic vision of an effective interchangeability of rôles. The rigidity of masculine and feminine rôles would automatically be weakened.

It is certain that at least up to the age of six, most children are convinced that women do nothing and that those who work outside the home do something so insignificant that it is hardly worth mentioning. Proof of this image of female work in children from three to six was given in a series of drawings gathered together from various nursery schools (I shall come back to these in more detail later). In these drawings the children only depict men who work and women who stay home – mothers. Only one in a hundred shows a woman who actually *leaves* the house to work, but one is not too sure where she is going nor exactly what she is going to do. Masculine activities, however, are always precisely characterised.

'Men all do dangerous things,' says a little boy from Bergéret's school, rather sententiously as he stands admiring a worker repairing a roof. The conclusion could well be: women all do insignificant things. This underlines the image of male and female work one hands down to children and which they have of its reality.

The majority of nursery school teachers – either because of their training or because of their personal qualities – are the last people to be able to offer a model for self-realisation which is different from the traditionally acceptable one. Having themselves had a conformist education, with which they are satisfied; ignorant of themselves and of the problems of the world around them; unaware of the privilege which the fact of taking care of children and being able to shape them into thinking, creative beings represents; devoid of any political or social commitment; repressed emotionally and sexually; frustrated and often disgusted by the work they do in which they do not sense the perspectives or importance; empty of vitality and degraded; victims of a segregation which abandons them to a ghetto where there are only women babbling senseless, melancholy statements with no trace of any innovatory breath; forgotten by those who are responsible for schools and pretend to reform them by starting from the top of the hierarchy rather than the base; imprisoned in their little lives woven with domestic banalities, they wearily drag through their mornings with the children and have as their main preoccupation that the children stay as immobile and silent as possible. Their reaction to the idea that men can teach in nursery school is scandalised stupefaction:

'It's not men's work. One needs a lot of patience with children and men don't have any' (this from a teacher who had lost her patience at least a dozen times during the course of a morning and who admitted that in her own family her father had been much more patient with the children than her mother).

'It's a feminine profession. Men have so many others among which to choose.'

'In Italy, men aren't interested in children. They don't take care of them. They bring home the pay packet and that's it.'

'Men aren't made to stay with children. It's the fault of the education they've had' (an education which they calmly continue to perpetuate, in home and school alike).

'Women have a special "innate" ability and they are more suited to being with children.'

'And then, why call it nursery school?' (revealing how the choice of terms reinforces prejudice).

'It's woman's work. One has to play mother to the child.'

'Perhaps some time in the future, even men will be able to teach in nursery school; but the moment hasn't yet come. It runs counter to all our habits' (as if habits couldn't be changed).

'Apart from the patience which men don't have, one needs a lot of intuition to understand children. Men aren't interested in understanding children.'

'Children would never accept a man as a teacher' (have they ever been asked?).

'Even if it were right, how would one make parents accept such a thing? Parents would never want to send their children to school with a man' (why, is never explained, but one senses that there are delicate moral issues at stake here).

'And why should we allow men to take even this work away from us?'

'If it were to teach the children gymnastics or something of that kind, all right. But a man is not really made to be a teacher. The work is too *delicate*.'

'A man with children! That would be altogether ridiculous.'

'Men are more authoritarian. They would *frighten* such young children. Women on the contrary are gentler. They are like their mothers.'

'I've sometimes brought my fiancé to classes. He likes little children a lot. But I can't see him as a teacher. He'd get bored immediately. Most of the time children are boring and one needs a lot of patience.'

'Well, as for this story of male nursery school teachers, I have really never heard anything said of it.'

Teachers who discriminate

How do such teachers establish a learning relationship with

children? Do they behave in the same way towards boys and girls or differently? And if this is the case, are they aware of it or not? What do they expect of either sex? How do boys and girls respond to this expectation on the teacher's part? As far as establishing a relationship with children is concerned, it seems that with a few exceptions we are a very long way from the model teacher described in the 'pedagogical directives' given to state nursery schools.

Speaking to teachers or observing them at work gives one reason to shudder. There is not the least difference between the very old teacher due to retire in a few months, and the young graduate who is just starting off. An old teacher reprimands a little girl of three for sucking her thumb. When the little girl, though conscious of the observation, continues in her 'pastime', the teacher threatens that one day she will see her thumb fall off. The same teacher intervenes to separate two fighting boys and asks them what has happened. The two children answer at the same time, 'It's him.' But the teacher must have followed the quarrel better than I did, for, sure of herself, she addresses one of the boys and says to him, 'I saw you. You started!' Wanting to demonstrate her omniscience and omnipresence, she answers the accused boy's protests of innocence with, 'Roberto, you're a liar, I saw you. It's your fault, you should know.' Raising her voice and signalling to Roberto to stand in front of her, she says, 'When Pinocchio told a lie, his nose grew and grew. When children tell lies, a black stain appears on their forehead.' The child, preoccupied, mechanically touches his forehead. 'Brush away your hair,' says the teacher, and turning towards the class who has not missed one word of this curious piece of training, she continues, 'You see, children, if Roberto has a black stain on his forehead.' All the children crane their necks to see. Tension has reached a paroxysm. Roberto is on the verge of tears, but resists. 'I know, I know, children,' the teacher concludes in an apocalyptic tone, 'You can't see the black stain on Roberto's forehead, because you're children, but the teacher can see it, because teachers see everything.' And satisfied with her pedagogic improvisation she sends Roberto back to his seat.

Another elderly teacher reminded a little girl in my presence of all the mischief she had done. She then said to me in a loud voice to make sure the child could hear, 'Do you know, Madam, that the other day Lisetta called her mother an idiot? She's a very bad little girl. Her tongue is well hung, but if she continues, some day

her tongue will fall out and she'll never be able to speak again.'
During this time Lisetta nervously twists a corner of her white
apron and balances herself on her toes giving sighs of great agitation. A slightly older little girl approaches Lisetta, puts her arm
round her and tries to take her away to console her. But the implacable teacher intervenes: 'Leave her. She has to stay alone to
think over her mischievous deeds!'

A nineteen-year-old trainee is sitting very straight at her desk.
She is clearly thinking of her own affairs. From time to time, she
smoothes her hair and graciously bats eyelashes on extravagantly
made-up eyes. She painfully and half-heartedly emerges from her
reverie when a child or the teacher ask her something. Questioned
about her future projects, she answers: 'That depends on my
fiancé; you know, he doesn't want me to work, and since we are
getting married next year, I don't know, we'll see.'

The immaturity of this response with its stress on the words
fiancé and marriage, makes one fearful and permits the girl's true
project to be seen.

I address myself to another young trainee, a nun, who is active,
alert, and continually worried about proposing new activities to
the children. It is impossible not to see in her apparent perfection
an astounding inner discipline which denies her all liberty or
spontaneity. It is precisely this conformity to an ideal model which
gives one hint of the enormous effort to repress herself on all levels
she must have had to make in order to reproduce such a model.
To behave like this is one thing; to have to constrain oneself to do
so is another. Her air of never imposing anything on the children,
when in fact she imposes everything, is an instrument for domination which is infinitely more subtle, dangerous, and aggressive than
the most overtly authoritarian manner. It does not permit the
children any openly aggressive and hence liberating reaction, but
rather provokes in them an incapacity to rebel and a sense of guilt.

Examples of such teachers could be multiplied many times over.
Nearly all of them use the concepts 'good' and 'bad'. Julietta is
good because she sits without moving at her desk as the teacher has
ordered. Maurizio is bad because he never stays in one place and
continually goes off to bother his friends. Little girls are good because they keep to their two-by-two file. Little boys are bad because
they always break ranks, nudge each other, etc. . . . The teacher's
judgment about a child's work never refers directly to the work –
'This time it's well done; this time it's less well done.' Rather it

harps back constantly to the child's person – 'good pupil; bad pupil'.

To direct questions about differences in boys' and girls' school behaviour, teachers united to agree that these exist and that they are significant. All of them repeat the same points. Boys are livelier, noiser, more aggressive and quarrelsome; less disciplined, more disobedient, greater liars and lazier. They apply themselves less to their work, write less well and less quickly. They are more disorderly, dirtier and less intelligent. On the other hand, they are more independent, need affection, approbation and help less; are more self-confident, show greater solidarity with their own sex, have a great sense of friendship, aren't traitors, don't babble and cry less. Little girls are more docile, more servile, more dependent on the teacher's judgment, weaker in character. They cry and gossip more, are greater tattle-tales, show less solidarity with their own sex and are less gay. They are more intelligent, methodical and organised; they apply themselves better; take better care of their personal appearance; are more obedient, obliging, loyal, careful and disciplined. The speed with which teachers will enumerate the faults and qualities of boys and girls betrays their habit of classifying children according to their sex and on a deeper level of discriminating in their behaviour towards them. If one were free of prejudice or if one were trying to be free, the correct answer to questions of this type would consist of distinguishing within a group of individuals those who are more aggressive, more orderly, more dependent, etc., with no reference to their sex. After all, there are little girls who are more aggressive than *some* little boys, and little boys more orderly than some little girls. Because of our conditioned response to sex stereotypes, these however become the exceptions, the 'deviants'.

The profound difference between men and women, already wholly apparent at nursery school age, reinforces the conviction that one is dealing with 'natural' phenomenon, with behaviour engendered by two different biological conditions. It is possible that biology does have something to do with the different behavioural patterns of men and women, but we will only be able to ascertain this once social conditioning according to sex has disappeared.

If one asks teachers what, according to them, is at the basis of the profound differences in behaviour between boys and girls, they will answer that one is dealing here with a 'natural, hereditary,

innate' factor. However, these same teachers betray a marked confusion on this score as well as a complex lack of reflection, when
they add to these adjectives such considerations as: 'Perhaps in
100 years boys and girls will be equal because the education of the
sexes is gradually growing uniform.'

Or speaking simultaneously of innate behaviour and conditioning which results from education within the family, they will recognise that parents' expectations are different for boys and girls,
and then go on to say that girls are more 'naturally' prone to get
married and have children than boys. They note that in class
boys will tend to sit with boys and girls with girls and they consider this to be spontaneous and natural. But those who have had
the opportunity to make comparisons because they have taught in
schools encompassing different social groupings, admit that this
phenomenon is much more pronounced in village or small town
schools where masculine and feminine stereotypes are more rigidly
differentiated. Finally one could say that they do nothing more
than expose a real phenomenon without realising that it constitutes an educational problem and considering that the situation could even partially be changed. These teachers, who occupy
the position most appropriate for changing the situation, allevi-
ating its strongest pressures and eliminating the most obvious instances of discrimination, do not even attempt to do so.

Caught in evident contradictions, they speak at the same time of
both 'the masculine and feminine nature' and of the different conditioning of the sexes within the family. Yet they refuse all responsibility and say, 'I treat them all the same way.' They do not
manifest even the slightest intention of changing anything. For
them all is well as it is. They are there for quite different reasons:
to maintain discipline, or 'prepare' children to enter school proper;
or to keep them from being lazily inert. Sometimes they are preoccupied by problems of teaching method but only to the extent
where this will produce more brilliant results. But they are
altogether ignorant of what children are or could be. They are
conservative to the full extent of the term and tend to reproduce
with no significant modification the very educational curricula,
relations, values and hierarchies they learned.

In the best of cases, they propose more modern educational
methods, try to be less authoritarian and instigate more democratic
relations with the children. However, in what they do there is not
the least attempt to analyse the educational relationship and what

it implies, not even a whiff of revolution. These are the daughters of a patriarchial society, its least rebellious daughters. They have fully swallowed the society's ideologies and they smile with commiseration when one speaks to them of female emancipation, since the existent male–female relationship suits them very well while the very idea of introducing some changes into it horrifies them. They are timid creatures who have chosen a profession which shelters them from many things in life which might be traumatic as well as stimulating and exciting.

It is at the nursery school level that family and teacher begin their game of thrusting responsibility for education on the other's shoulders. In this pitch and catch of real and supposed mistakes, the greatest mistake is not even considered: that of stifling the energy, creativity and vitality of little girls and favouring aggression and the competitive spirit in little boys. What does this signify? Are men and women not always profoundly different? Certainly they do not suddenly become different at an adult age but are already so when they are little. And one continues to hear: that's natural, don't they need to be complementary in order to get along? If they are equal, there's a danger that they may hold no more attractions for one another. They are different physically; why shouldn't they also be so psychologically? And without making the contradictions apparent, teachers accept as a necessity all the limits imposed on little girls – for it is understood that: 'This will help them when they have their own family', or 'They are happier this way', or 'They are weak and need more affection', or 'The dangers are greater for little girls than for boys' (what danger?).

In effect, what first strikes one when one walks into a nursery school classroom is that the children are working or playing in groups of the same sex. Since they are free to move about and change places, this might seem to be a spontaneous choice. If one asks teachers if this division by sex is induced in any way, they answer that it's quite spontaneous and add that, on the contrary, they would prefer mixed groups so that the children 'could learn to get along with each other, for then the boys grow less wild and aggressive and the girls less weepy'. This affirmation corresponds to the truth insofar as no teacher has probably ever said, 'Boys must sit at the tables on the right, girls on the left'; or 'It is forbidden for boys to play with girls.' But in one way or another, teachers communicate to children a fundamental fear of either their being too numerous or getting along too well, a fear which is in fact the fear of sexual games. The objective of separating the sexes can be reached in many ways, but the principal one is to consider the two sexes as distinct groups by turning them into rivals and accentuating their behavioural differences: 'Today the boys were better than the girls.' 'Look how well the girls have tidied up.' 'How can you always make so much noise? Look how obedient the girls are.' Teachers also use methods which not only make the groups antagonistic, but inculcate attitudes of fear and mutual mistrust as if the two were enemies and incapable of meeting and understanding one another. 'Don't go and play with the boys, you know they'll hurt you.' 'You won't come and complain, if they push you. You know what little boys are like.' Little boys who might wish to play with girls are discouraged in even more efficient fashion. Here the ploy of ridicule is used and they are given to understand that female games are degrading to them. The objective of persuading boys that little girls are inferior and contemptible beings and of persuading little girls of the same thing is reached. At this level, separation is already irremediable. Few children will try to break through the imposed barrier. It is not only the adults' criticism which prevents them, but also that of their peers who, having accepted the division as law, have a vested interest in maintaining it and imposing conformity on all others.

Observation reveals marked differences of behaviour in the two groups. The boys are openly wilder and noiser, as if they were caught up in a continual agitation which enfolds any proposed activities. The girls are more placid and quieter. They are more prone to being spectators than protagonists – of what happens in class, of what the boys do. The reaction to my presence in classes is characteristic. Teachers usually introduce me as 'a lady who is to stay with us a few days'. Boys only look at me briefly and somewhat distractedly, neither commenting nor asking questions – as if the event has no interest for them – and then return to their activities. The girls' groups on the other hand are a mass of whispers. They are filled with curiosity and an excitement which is hard to contain. It manifests itself in long glances which shift in order not to meet my eyes, low-voiced commentaries on my clothes, my looks, what I'm doing: real gossips at their windows. Some girls immediately leave the games, which have absorbed them until then, and chin in hand contemplate me. Others circle round me with no apparent aim in mind, except perhaps that of approaching me later after they have made long detours to observe me more closely and to place themselves in my field of vision.

In this specific case, the fundamental difference between boys and girls was that the first in no way considered the question of how they might or might not please me. Nor did they try to verify the success of the impression they had made on me. The girls – with the exceptions of the 'different' ones, that is, the less 'feminine', more intelligent and independent ones – abandoned whatever they were doing to submit themselves of their own free will to my consideration and estimation. They were trying to please me and obtain some confirmation from me. Once again their behaviour led to the question, 'What impression am I making?'

In suburban schools, behaviour which is considered typical of the two sexes is much more pronounced than in big city schools. This is of course because the models offered the children are much more differentiated, clear-cut, and limited. For example, boys play at being 'tough'. They make menacing and challenging gestures. Little girls, hands on hips, swing their behinds as they walk, toss their locks and spend hours brushing each other's hair. They talk endlessly, with complicity and satisfaction, about clothes and jewellery, embarking on long descriptions from which they derive an evident narcissitic pleasure. They already know how to remove a part of their energy and interests from external reality in order to concentrate on the external aspects of their own person. They have already learned to what degree appearance and beauty are important to women. Though their interest in others seems to be greater than the little boys', it is not in fact a real interest, but rather a need to examine different models so that they can imitate the most desirable. This is a definitive manifestation of a lack of self-confidence and of a need to be continually reassured. Precisely because the little girl's ego is weaker (she is granted less independence, considered less important, and is less often asked to realise herself) she needs continual reassurance from without in order to know whether she is or is not living up to others' expectations.

Sexual segregation: little girls in the service of boys

In traditional nursery schools, the toilet ritual precedes the mid-morning snack. All the children, whether they want to or not, are taken off to wee. The ritual begins with the teacher's announcement: 'Children, let's go to the toilets, double file, girls in front,

L.G.—5

boys at the back.' And the children are separated into pairs according to sex. The file moves along the corridor towards the toilet
door and the children are sent in to wee, two by two, sex by sex.
Little girls in twos until they have all had their turn and then little
boys in twos. After the toilets, it is time for a snack and then into
the playground for play. Once again the row is formed according
to the same rules and the children trek out into the playground
where, with few exceptions, they play in groups divided according
to sex.

When the children in a class are artificially divided in this way
for several months or years, it becomes impossible for them not
to feel categorised as a group. How are they not to make of this
continual division an iron law from which they cannot escape –
especially since it is imposed or suggested, directly or indirectly,
by a thousand other features of their daily lives?

After the age of three, they actually *do* begin to feel more comfortable with children of their own sex. Male and female have been
brought up in such opposed ways that they *have* become effectively
different and can find no satisfactory manner for being together.
They complain, each in their own turn, of their respective faults
and find the other sex quite insufferable. Only after puberty will
they meet again on common ground, but the sexual tie will remain
the only one which brings them together, since for a thousand
other reasons they will continue not to understand one another
and to feel like strangers.

The need to categorise human beings at all costs is always based
on the most elementary, the most evident divisions – sex, race, age,
religion, etc. First and most fundamental of all categories is that
of sex: it constitutes a form of racism, but since it seems so
natural, it permits no suspicion to arise concerning its injustice or
falsehood. Far from being a natural fact, division according to
sex is actually a cultural fact. It is indispensable for maintaining
certain recognised privileges which belong to those who have established and inexorably perpetuated this discrimination throughout
history, namely men, aided and abetted of course by women's complicity and passive acceptance.

Let us suppose that, instead of the classification laid down on the
'natural' bases of sex and race, a society had classified personality
on the basis of eye-colour. It had decreed that all blue-eyed people
were gentle, submissive and responsive to the needs of others, and
all brown-eyed people were arrogant, dominating, self-centred and

purposive. In this case two complementary social themes would be women together – the culture, in its art, its religion, its formal personal relations would have two threads instead of one. There would be blue-eyed men and blue-eyed women which would mean that there were gentle 'maternal' women and gentle 'maternal' men. A blue-eyed man might marry a woman who had been bred to the same personality as himself, or a brown-eyed woman who had been bred to the contrasting personality. One of the strong tendencies that makes for homosexuality, the tendency to love the similar rather than the antithetical person, would be eliminated. Hostility between the two sexes as groups would be minimised since the individual interests of members of each sex could be woven together in different ways, and marriages of similarity and friendships of contrast need carry no necessary handicap of possible psycho-sexual maladjustment. The individual would still suffer a mutilation of his temperamental preferences, for it would be the unrelated fact of eye-colour that would determine the attitudes which he was educated to show. Every blue-eyed person would be forced into submissiveness and declared maladjusted if he or she showed any traits that it had been decided were only appropriate to the brown-eyed. The greatest social loss, however, in the classification of personality on the basis of sex would not be present in this society which based its classification on eye-colour. Human relations, and especially those which involve sex, would not be artificially distorted.

But such a course, the substitution of eye-colour for sex as a basis upon which to educate children into groups showing contrasting personalities, while it would be a definite advance upon a classification by sex, remains a parody of all the attempts that society has made through history to define an individual's rôle in terms of sex, or colour, or date of birth or shape of head.[4]

As we have stated, women are conditioned to like placing themselves at the service of men. For the conditioning to bear fruit, it must begin early. In the family, it starts at an extremely young age. It is then reinforced and stabilised in the nursery school.

Let us look at a few examples. The mid-morning snack will illustrate the automatism with which teachers and children themselves conform to certain patterns already assimilated by both. Theoretically, each child should get his little basket, place his napkin on the table at the place he has chosen, and put his snack on it. In practice, few boys do this. Most of them take their time, wander about from one place to another, while the disciplined little girls go and fetch their baskets and sit down in their places to eat. The teacher urges the boys to do the same, repeating her invitation several times, but to no avail. Disorder continues and rather than allowing things to take their own course and accepting that a child who is not sufficiently independent or sufficiently hungry to get his own snack will quite happily do without, the teacher finds a simple and for her more practical solution. She sends one or more little girls to get Stefano and Paulo's baskets; then 'they will perhaps sit down and we shall all have some peace!'

There is an implicit indulgence towards boys in this teacher's attitude. 'They must be taken as they are.' And the little girls do not need to be urged to do so. They have already had innumerable examples at home of the way in which one makes life easier and more agreeable for boys. The mother or the sisters do everything in order to have the table set on time. Should the latter show any recalcitrance they have it repeated to them over and over that they must conform to this custom, that it is only by serving men that one fine day they will be 'chosen' by them. Praise is women's only reward. The effect which their behaviour will have constantly preoccupies them and they have an enormous need to be loved and accepted because they are already conscious of their inferiority. They must please. It is an imperative.

The teacher in this example avoids interfering directly and doing what the little boys refuse to do or do only unwillingly. This could undermine her authority. Instead she resolves the issue by calling on the little girls for help. No one is scandalised by so little. Yet there is racism inherent in this behaviour which passes unnoticed. People who are generally sensitive to other aspects of racism are untouched by such a typical instance: a being who is considered inferior is being made to serve another who is considered to be superior. If we transform the proposition and suppose that in a class of three to five-year-olds there are black and white children and the same situation arises – the teacher asks the docile, submissive blacks to set the table for the whites ... Everyone would be horrified!

Let us think for a moment of the kind of racism which exists in Italy and imagine that a similar situation occurs in a class made up of southern and northern children. Inevitably the children in the two groups would conclude that they were different, that adults did not want them to stay together and that they expect different kinds of behaviour from each group.

Little girls lend themselves to utilitarian tasks which serve boys each time the need arises in a class to put things away or clean up. Alternately the responsibility of disturbing things is voluntarily taken on by boys, since this confers authority upon them. In some cases, the teacher will directly order little girls to 'put away the construction toys'. In other cases, she will ask, 'Who is going to put away the toys?' – and it is then that acquired reflexes come into play. The little boy will take on the distracted air of someone who has decided to participate as little as possible in the drudgery and who is taking time out to see how the situation will resolve itself. If a teacher occasionally insists that the boys pick up the toys, they will get up lazily, making as much of a commotion as possible, and spend a long time over the task still leaving half the things scattered here and there. The result is disappointing. 'They do it so unwillingly and so badly, that finally I don't ask them any more,' admits one teacher. This is precisely what the boys wanted, just the result they counted on. The teacher's need to have the class function smoothly and have order maintained rests on the willing collaboration of little girls. After her first few disappointments with boys, incompatible with her sense of order, the teacher will only address herself to little girls. It is enough for such episodes to be repeated a few times for little girls to intervene automatically. But if a teacher were to take her courage in her hands and state clearly that each and every child must be independent and not exploit others, she would win the battle once and for all and initiate a more just way of living together in the classroom.

Such behaviour is reproduced in other circumstances. A child running across the classroom falls and hurts his knee. The teacher tells him to go to the washroom to clean himself and then to come back so she can bandage his leg. At the same time she tells a little girl to accompany him, since otherwise, 'who knows what Alberto will get up to alone in the toilet'. She says this in a somewhat flattering tone – one that is *never* used on girls – and which suggests that the child is given to engaging in heavens knows what kind of exciting games in that unwelcoming place. When I ask this teacher why she doesn't have Alberto accompanied by another boy, she answers that she personally would do this, but that the principal does not like two boys to go to the toilet together because 'they always end up by fighting and disturbing other classes'. Then why not send the child alone? 'Because I feel less worried if there's a little girl there; they know what's up and *voluntarily* do these little services for one. It makes them feel *important*.' In effect,

these 'little services' multiply. 'Tie Carletto's shoelaces' – though
Carletto can quite well tie them himself, if no one comes to help
him. 'Give Stephano a tissue so he can blow his nose. *His mother
forgot to give him one this morning.*' 'Go and take care of your
little brother who's crying and wipe his nose.' 'Who is the little girl
who will wipe the water off the floor?' 'There are some construction pieces left under Giagio's desk; Antonietta, will you put them
away?' And so on.

For a teacher to tell little boys to do similar services for little
girls is, however, inconceivable. If we try to reverse the rôles in
these stories, we have a sense of displacement. One doesn't ask
little boys to wipe their little sisters' noses, clean up for them or
tie their shoe-laces.

A little girl picks up two luncheon baskets (a pink one for girls,
a blue one for boys) and prepares to set the table for herself and
her brother. The snack consists largely of pizza which the girl
divides into two unequal parts hoping to keep the larger one for
herself. The little boy protests. He wants it all. The teacher intervenes and asks the girl to give the larger part to her brother 'because he is smaller'. The little girl appears not to notice and starts
to eat impassively. But the teacher insists. Disappointed, the little
girl takes a piece of her share and without a word gives it to her
brother – thus attempting to reestablish justice. The little boy
calms down. The teacher comments, 'you're hardly generous', and
the little girl blushes, betraying how much the remark has hurt her.
Once she has finished, she gets up to put away her basket. Her
brother, absorbed in a comic book, has not even thought of this.
On my request, the teacher asks the little boy to tidy his place and
put away his basket. He looks at her as if she has gone quite
mad, refuses with a categorical 'no' and returns to his comic. Then
the little girl, without having been asked, but interpreting my request in this way (and out of a need to respond to others' wishes)
and still under the influence of the teacher's remark quickly cleans
up and puts away the blue basket. She has the satisfied look of
someone who is certain of obtaining approval.

Spontaneously two little girls take hold of a pail and start to
clean the tables with a sponge. The first uses the sponge with
nervous rapid gestures, as if to prove her efficiency. The second,
with teeth clenched and an obsessed air, slowly draws circles on
the table taking care not to leave an inch unscrubbed – the scrupulous care of a phobic child. Observing the activity of girls, one

often gets the feeling that it is not an ?nd in itself – as it is for younger children and most often boys – but that the desire to please others has already in part substituted the pleasure of doing, acting, producing and testing oneself. It is this which removes from activity that creative aspect which it should include.

A little boy goes out to the toilet. He doesn't shut the class door properly and it begins to bang. After looking at the door questioningly for a while, a little girl gets up decidedly and goes to close it. The teacher thanks her. Not one boy had shown the least reaction to the banging door.

The teacher calls two little girls to her desk to give them the work materials planned for the afternoon. They are very proud of their responsibility, return to their seats and with little jerky gestures readjust their skirts over their knees. They exchanged pleased looks of complicity. One is reminded of two little old ladies.

The conditioning of little girls towards serving boys and adults in general, as well as the pressure exerted on them so that their affection is never distracted but rather directed towards resolving banal practical problems, displaces an important part of their vital energy. Rather than engaging in games, creative enterprise, or free activity which might be an end in itself and result in fulfilment of their own personality, they are kept busy with activities which serve the group as a whole.

Energy, however, does not come on order. One uses as much as one has. It can be channelled into positive enriching directions, or be dispersed and destroyed. This phenomenon is plainly visible in adult working women. Despite the passion, enthusiasm and ambition they put into their work, much of their energy is taken up by domestic worries and chores: shopping, organising the household, planning lunches, dinners, caring for husband and children when they are ill, etc. These tasks fall on all working women's shoulders and no one is prepared to take them on in their place. The constant swing of their thought and energy from one pole to its opposite – something men do not experience – prevents them from mobilising all their strength to one purpose. In truth, they must above all be prepared to serve and only if they have sufficient energy left over, can they use this to realise themselves as productive individuals.

Why should a little girl be preoccupied with closing a banging door when a boy does not even notice it? Is it that it is more interesting and amusing to close a door than to play a game or finish a drawing? Certainly not. And how, if not by conditioning, does one reach the point where a little girl of five turns her attention away from what she is doing in order to get up to close a door for the common good. She should be reproached for having abandoned something important for something unimportant. But no, she is thanked and in this way her inferiority is underlined. It often happens that little girls spontaneously put themselves at the service of little boys to help them in games in which they do not themselves participate directly. Such an attitude already reveals their interest and envy for a male world from which they feel excluded.

Examples: A little girl playing with plasticine takes care from time to time to knead her friend's modelling clay in order to soften it.

Another, without having been asked, gets up to fill a beaker of water for her little friend who is painting.

A third abandons her work to console a little boy who is crying. She puts her arm round him and says, 'Don't cry, Bruno.'

A fourth slips under the table to pick up construction kit units and returns them to the little boy who has dropped them.

It would be much more agreeable to see boys and girls both doing things for one another. But I have never yet seen this happen. Boys' indifference with respect to what happens to girls is total. It is a symptom of the egocentricity which reinforces their education and in this it is quite unlike that of little girls.

The behaviour of girls and boys is quite as characteristic when they want to get something from one another. A little boy will charge into a group of girls and amidst a chorus of female protests will grab a few plastic units and dash back to his place. A girl who needs a few plastic units to finish a structure she has been ardently working on will approach a group of boys with a battery of charming smiles, simpers and coquettish gestures and thus obtain a handful of units. In neither case does the teacher intervene. She has probably not noticed anything – though she might in other cases intervene to reprimand the boy's aggression and not the seductive hypocrisy of the little girl.

This resource to seduction in order to obtain things is not only accepted in little girls, but encouraged. Never is there any attempt made to correct them and to suggest a more appropriate and dignified manner in which demands might be made. Similarly the interventions made to correct little boys' excessive aggression are often ambivalent. They reveal a secret predisposition on the teacher's part; a suitable mixture of unconscious compliance and admiration for an audacity she finds seductive. Fundamentally, this is the way the teachers prefer men – determined and insolent – and she silently rejoices over the fact that the boys are on the right path.

Frederico, a beautiful lively child, finds himself reprimanded by the teacher for having tripped another boy. Yet he is the first to be called to the teacher's desk when the drawing paper is distributed. This amounts to an apology from the teacher for the reprimand she was forced to make earlier. This contradictory attitude shows just how much classical male aggression is accepted as a norm of behaviour.

In special training centres (such as the Montessori schools),[5] where there is no distinction made in the activities available to the two sexes, one can still see instances of discrimination. These may be more subtle but they are equally alienating. One example lies in the division of duties related to serving dining-room lunches. In an educational bulletin for 'constructive and practical activities'[6] an article on 'Serving at Table' states:

> In the group there is also a *headwaiter*, waiters and waitresses. These last stand near the table while the waiters walk to and fro between the tables, the service table where the headwaiter remains, and the kitchen.

In this case, the highest ranking position in a collective kind of work is reserved for a man. Where there are waiters and waitresses, the first are given the tasks which require movement – corresponding to the image of man as the active one – and have the greater responsibility attached to them. The waitresses are given the stationary rôle which thrusts woman back to her image of passivity. The article continues: 'Each waiter, having had a plate put on his tray, goes towards the table where a waitress is waiting.' Where clearing the tables is concerned, 'the waiter pushes the trolley round', while the waitress places the dirty dishes on it.

This may not seem a very significant example. It is cited here to demonstrate that in nursery schools where above all else one seeks to respect the individuality of each child, one ends up by reproducing, quite unconsciously, the habitual models of the active, 'managerial' boy and the passive, subordinate girl.

Preferred activities and proposed activities

Where the activities preferred by boys and by girls are concerned, teachers insist that the differences between the sexes is marked. Boys, for instance, prefer games of movement, construction, clay modelling and drawing. Girls prefer sewing, making paper cut-outs, playing shopkeeper – but they also like clay work, construction and drawing. Here too one can easily discern teachers' influence, though they insist that they do not intervene to guide the children's choice. For example, a teacher will distribute plastic figures such as Indians and cowboys on horseback, soldiers, cars, missiles with astronauts, etc. to little boys doing clay modelling. She does not give any such objects to little girls so that they too can enrich their clay work; or if she goes give them some, the objects are different – cows, hens, lambs, cats, children, trees, fences. To justify herself, the teacher will say that it is the children themselves who prefer one thing to another. She recognises this and merely satisfies their expectation. Yet the game of cutting up paper and assembling little boxes is proposed only to girls, not to boys. The teacher has nothing against giving a group of girls a large box filled with a confusion of wreaths and comets to disentangle. But she avoids proposing the same activity to boys. 'They'd make a right mess of it! . . .'

As for playing at shopkeeper, this is never even mentioned to boys. Should a boy be attracted by this game, he is openly dissuaded from taking part in it. It is worth citing the example of Giorgetto here, a gentle boy, about five years old, and the pupil of an old, tired teacher.

Giorgetto is much better behaved than many boys in his class and than some girls as well. He is not particularly aggressive, but neither does he allow himself to be stepped upon. He works continually in a group or alone. The teacher declares that boys and girls like staying in their own groups, that girls prefer dolls and dressing up, while boys prefer cars or construction games. She goes on to state that girls are always rejected by boys if they fancy participating in their games; but that girls are often quite happy to let boys join in their games. Yet this teacher declares that she has nothing to do with this state of affairs and that she exercises no pressure on the children.

The teacher then invites *the little girls* to form a group around several tables and she gives them the necessary equipment for playing shop. The little girls respond enthusiastically. The boys seem to detach themselves wholly except for Giorgetto: hands behind his back, stomach jutting forward, he looks like someone who is perplexed by a serious problem. He observes the girls from a distance without going to approach them. Although he is dying to participate in the girls' game, he already knows – probably because he has tried before or seen his friends do so – that this is not considered to be a boy's game. Yet he can't help being irresistibly attracted to it and he approaches the teacher and asks in a voice so strangled that he must repeat himself, if he can play with the girls.

'With the girls!' the teacher repeats, scandalised. She takes the child by the shoulders – as if she had suddenly been struck by shame and pity for him – and embraces him. The child blushes, visibly embarrassed and tries to extricate himself with dignity by stating in an uncertain voice, 'But I wanted to be the supplier?'

He hangs on to this compromise which would permit him to participate in the little girls' game in a rôle which is seen to be masculine. His tormented air clearly reflects the effort this attempt to save face, to preserve his self-esteem vis-à-vis the teacher and especially his own peer group, is costing him. But the teacher obstinately remains the prisoner of her own mental apparatus which obliges her to struggle within a simple situation which she herself has confounded 'They already have their suppliers,' she tells Giorgetto. 'Well, I'll bring the eggs then,' Giorgetto bravely insists. The teacher glances rapidly in my direction. I don't know what conclusion she draws from my impassive spectator's air. Sighing and with a little embarrassed laugh, she says, 'Girls, Giorgetto wants to play with you. He wants to be the supplier.' The girls who have not missed a word of the interchange, though they go on looking busy, weighing chick peas, green peas, rice, do not deign to pay the least attention to their poor friend.

Giorgetto is on the verge of tears; but his niceness must hide a good degree of stubbornness, for he approaches the girls and waits, hands in the pockets of his apron. The girls continue to ignore him. He is on the point of collapse, his smile grows shaky, he stands on one foot, then the other and grinds away at the bottoms of his pockets. Finally, one little girl addresses him with an authoritative voice: 'Mr Supplier, I need some potatoes.' Giorgetto, who has resigned himself to the worst, jumps with surprise and joy and flies to the back of the class from where he quickly returns, his hands loaded with imaginary potatoes.

The teacher passes in front of me and comments: 'You see how difficult it is to get them to play together? They really don't want to.' She is quite unaware that she herself has provoked the entire situation and is convinced that she has given an example of a spontaneous phenomenon.

Giorgetto's case must not be seen as that of a gentle little boy who prefers quiet girls' games to the more aggressive ones of his own sex. In certain schools, as for instance the Montessori schools, the same activities are offered to children of both sexes, ironing, washing or dishwashing, sweeping, setting the table. Those who have observed the children's activities have noted that children of both sexes choose these activities with the same enthusiasm. This does not lead to any particular conflicts and still less to sexual deviation.

Another teacher gives a command. 'Girls, go and get the drawings we did yesterday morning.' Paulo, who from all appearances has only heard the end of this instruction, follows the group of girls. The teacher laughs and makes fun of him, 'Paulo, are you a girl too? Then we'll put a ribbon in your hair.' Paulo turns scarlet, lowers his head confusedly, and returns to his place where he sits for a long time silent and perturbed. The girls look at him and snicker, while the boys laugh outright. Because of the teacher's comment, Paulo has lost a great deal of his male prestige. He has declassed himself – and the girls while making fun of him for his mistake, implicitly recognise their own inferiority. Just a little later, Paulo cries. A friend has taken a construction unit from him. Doubtlessly he would have been less quick to cry, if he hadn't suffered a previous frustration. But two families within a few minutes were too much. The implacable teacher continues to torment him: 'What kind of a boy is this cry-baby? Aren't you even capable of getting your toy back?' Completely humiliated, Paulo makes himself very small on his chair. He will not move for the rest of the morning – out of fear, no doubt, of exposing himself yet again.

Examples of teachers intervening in children's choice of activities 'appropriate' to their sex and thereby perpetuating discrimination and division between the sexes, could be multiplied into infinity. I ask a teacher, who declares that she totally respects the children's choices, what materials she would get for her class if a certain sum were placed at her disposal. She answers that she would make one corner of the class into a kitchen so that the girls could have a corner all to themselves. Then, after a moment's thought, she adds if the boys felt like going there, *she certainly wouldn't object*.

'As far as you're concerned, boys don't like to cook?'

'Yes, certainly, but not when they're young. They never do it (one doesn't know what gives her the authority to conclude this). My father is a very good cook, while my mother does very little cooking. *But he learnt when he was already quite well on in life.*'

One senses in her words a fear that in permitting boys to do domestic work, she might be exposing them to a loss of virility – supreme myth in regard of which she is prepared to sacrifice the most elementary commonsense. When they are grown-up they can cook, if they feel like it, all they like. In any case, they will be cooking 'as men', which means, in fact, that they can always rely on the women of the house to take care of the unpleasant aspects of the business. By then, too, their virility will have long been established. And, of course, teachers will then have nothing to do with it all. For the moment their duty is to make sure that they make these boys into 'real men'.

A teacher is distributing plastic units of various sizes, shapes and colours to both boys and girls. The boys assemble distinct shapes with which they simulate a plane in flight, imitating the roar of the engine, or they construct cars which they run over the tables. They show their creations to the teacher with declarations of: 'It's a jet, it's a Ferrari. This is Apollo XIII.' When a little girl constructs a magnificently complex structure which differs not at all from the boys and shows it to the teacher, the latter without waiting for the girl's interpretation or asking for one, says, 'That's nice. Is it a child? The structure looks like anything but a child. Perplexed for a moment, the little girl looks at the object in her hand – which for her probably represents something quite different, though she hasn't been given the opportunity to say so – and says 'Yes'. The girl learns that she is expected to construct only children, carriages and kitchens; and if she risks making an aeroplane, for example, the teacher, as well as all the other children, would look upon her suspiciously. Who would have the courage to withstand this look? When one feels that one belongs to the 'second sex', it takes a great deal of strength and self-assurance to withstand the criticism of others. Thus girls and women conform to what is expected of them: they do, say and behave according to the wishes of others. When the little girl, still worried and perplexed and holding her plastic structure, passes in front of me, I ask her, 'What is it?' She answers me uncertainly, 'I don't know.'

There is no need to explain to what extent this kind of reductive intervention by the adult – repeated in a thousand other circumstances and ways – creates an obstacle to creativity which is very difficult to overcome.

As a solution to a difficult moment, a teacher proposes a game of 'Wolf and Lambs'. Two children chase each other: the one fleeing is the Lamb; the one chasing, the Wolf. At the teacher's command, the rôles are to be changed. The teacher makes the children sit in two rows facing each other. Once again boys and girls are separated. First she calls two boys, then two more. The little girls are the silent spectators of masculine prowess. Some are tensely attentive and follow the game; others talk quietly. One is carefully brushing a friend's hair. The third group of boys is called. At this moment, the message transmitted by the teacher leaves no doubt. This is a boys' game. Despite this a little girl, as courageous as Giorgetto had been, comes forward and asks the teacher if she can run with Pierluigi. She wants to be the wolf. The teacher, stupefied, starts to laugh, exclaiming, 'But you are a girl, you can't chase after a boy?' Disappointed, the little girl goes back to her seat. Finally, after several boys have had their turn, the teacher has two girls run. They are less quick than the boys, but more ingenious in their pretence and feints. To finish off, the teacher has a boy and girl run. In this case, the little girl is beaten. But it would have been fairer to allow each child from the very beginning of the game to choose their wolf and their lamb. Each one would probably instinctively have chosen the right partner by evaluating his own strength and that of the adversary.

By conducting the game in this way, separating boys from girls, forcing girls to be spectators of active play, the teacher intimated that this was to be seen as a boys' game. By refusing the only little girl brave enough to dare set herself up against a boy; by allowing little girls to play only at the end as if she were making a concession to them and actually thought them unequal to the game; and finally by choosing the partners herself, this teacher was once again reproducing the whole gamut of alienating interventions we have examined until now. Once again, the fact of belonging to one sex rather than another served as a priori criteria of the ability and aptitude of each.

An important aspect of this game, as of so many others, must not be neglected: the identification which the child experiences with the interpreted character. The free choice of one or the other of the characters, the wolf or the lamb, the hunter or the hunted, the strong or the weak, permits the children to act out some of their own unexpressed problems and move beyond them. During the game, the terrorised expression of the child-lamb-hunted and the ferocious air of the wolf-hunter were explicit.

The children were living the rôle of the victim or that of his persecutor. Both of these correspond to a profound need in the child to enact certain fears, anxieties, aggressive and sadistic drives, which through the medium of dramatisation are made less offensive but nonetheless have a liberating impact. As far as little girls are concerned, why not have allowed those who felt the need to affirm a certain aggression and activity, the possibility of freely identifying with the wolf? This is the freedom which should be given to children: that of making a choice based on their own personal and individual needs. Instead children are forced to adhere to stereotyped models produced by our culture. In the name of these models we are sacrificing – with no positive goal in view – precious human qualities and energies which can belong indiscriminately to one or the other sex.

What drawings confirm

Examination of a considerable number of drawings collected from various nursery schools clearly reveals that from the age of five onwards there exist separate 'feminine' and 'masculine' worlds. The teachers who collected this material – the fruit of the children's daily activity – noted the contents as described by the children themselves in the margins of the drawings.

The little girls' drawings refer almost exclusively to events related to the daily life of the family. Few characters appear and these accomplish only insignificant acts. Mothers return home to cook; little girls bring eggs to grandmothers who are either ill or healthy; girls go for walks without any particular goal or to pray in church or to play with a friend. Others pick flowers for their mother, sing, play ring o' roses, return home to meet their little sisters or because they have found the cat. The home is always there in the forefront. The girls are either there, or have just left it, or come back to it. Mothers too are often present, but fathers appear more rarely.

Imaginative drawings are relatively rare. The ones that exist are mostly inspired by tales the girls have heard: the witch who gives Snow White the poisoned apple, the flowers which withered in the

fairies' house; Santa Claus bringing children presents. A limited
suffocating world, an uneventful family life and a fantasy life
which is equally poor. Taken as a whole, these drawings present a
faithful chronicle of the little girls' days – days which are regu-
lated by family habits which are themselves ordered by the social
group of which the family is part.

The poorest, most monotonous content in all these collected
drawings is to be found in those made by suburban little girls. In
these families, little girls, apart from going to nursery school
(where they are usually taken by their mothers despite the short
distances and almost total lack of danger), are kept at home to 'provide company' for their mothers. Even at this early age, the girls
help their mothers in the house. They rarely go out unaccompan-
ied, and if they do, it is to go to the corner shop, an errand which
can only take a few minutes. Most often, little girls go out with
their mothers. If they are permitted to play outside it is with the
injunction not to stray too far. They seldom take part in groups –
even those made up solely of other girls – tend to do things in
twos, either with their sister or a little friend. It is unthinkable
that they be allowed to play in mixed groups, and in any case, the
boys would refuse this.

Boys are granted infinitely more freedom. At the same age, they
have their own gang and often wander far from home without
adult surveillance. No one seems to worry about this. Boys' participation in household tasks or in running errands is non-existent.
They are not asked to do such things.

The majority of little girls' drawings have female subjects, but
more than a third contain male characters. In these latter cases,
the events depicted are much more varied and attractive. Indeed,
if anything in the least extraordinary happens in these drawings,
males are the subjects of the action. For example, father and son
go to a café; farmers pick apples; fishermen go off to sea; a cowboy rides a horse; a policeman conducts traffic; a father takes his
son for a jaunt in his pram; two boys open an umbrella because it
is going to rain. Not only are the more exciting and rare events
experienced only by boys, but these always take place outside the
home. Among all these pictures there was only one in which a little
girl depicted a *woman* waiting to board a ship. The teacher in
question had never before seen a little girl draw a boat and more-
over a boat in relation to a woman. She was amazed! The little
girl was certainly an exceptional case. Even when girls do draw

policemen conducting traffic or builders repairing roofs – since girls do after all notice the reality around them and despite their sedentary domestic existence they are neither deaf nor blind – they perceive these as outsiders. The girls know that these figures are not directly part of their lives and will never be so. They have to force themselves to describe such figures. Since none of them can imagine becoming policemen or builders, they cannot identify with these models. The girls delegate to the male all that they are not permitted to do because they are female. In this sense, their drawings are a faithful chronicle of the reality they live. The un-avoidable identification with a mother who is deaf and blind to all that is not related to home and family, plays a powerful rôle in their ability to distinguish between what should be and what should not be desired.

The subjects of the boys' pictures are infinitely richer and more varied than those of the little girls. Rarely limited to domestic life, these drawings depict scenes which have as their protagonists lorry drivers, policemen, workers, fishermen, gold-diggers, racing-car drivers, masons, Indians, shepherds, as well as the imaginary figures such as princes, magicians and phantoms. In these drawings, female figures are rare. From time to time one finds a mother looking for her daughter, sewing clothes for her son or taking him to school. Of the two little girls depicted, one is going home to eat fruit (what else can a girl do but go home?) while the other plays ring o' roses. Only one picture shows a woman getting out of a car and going to work. This solitary drawing of a woman *going* to work, unique among the many drawings of men *at work*, is significant of the way in which both boys and girls perceive female labour.

For them it does not exist. It would seem that boys of four and five only pay minimum attention to the female world, since only a few drawings have female characters. If one looks more closely at the names on these drawings, it becomes apparent that all the little boys' drawings with women in them have been done by a single boy. He, too, obviously constitutes an exception.

Girls, like boys, when they depict male figures at play, most often situate the action outside the home. But while the girls' rep-resentation always take place within 'permitted' territory, the action of the boys' pictures often unfolds in unorthodox locations. A little boy plays at war by throwing stones, another makes a game out of stamping on flowers.

Boys' games are described most often with great precision: they play at cops and robbers; a little boy hides behind a tree; two boys play on a football field, compete at flippers; play hide and seek in a meadow; a little boy runs his train across a garden; another plays with stones; two boys play pitch and catch. Within the home, the games are equally defined: miniature cars, tin soldiers, construction. One little boy builds a house; two others play at 'aeroplane'. Not the least sign of boys and girls playing together.

In girls' drawings, the theme of play occurs much less frequently. Little girls obviously 'play' less than boys. Even in their drawings, games are clearly defined only if they are played by boys. If girls are depicted, the games become vague and indeterminate, probably because girls' games largely imitate family life, that is, playing at being grown-ups. Boys, by preference, play 'with something'; girls play 'at something'.

Through these drawings, one understands how little girls see themselves, boys, and the world around them. While boys almost wholly ignore girls, they, on the contrary, are spectators who observe boys, are sometimes envious of their freedom, prowess and supremacy; sometimes indifferent, because they have already perfectly adapted to their feminine condition. The attitude which is revealed by the drawings confirms what we already noted within nursery schools. While boys pay almost no attention to girls and are implicitly contemptuous of them, girls pay a great deal of attention to boys which implies both admiration and envy.

By the age of five, then, everything is already settled. The appropriation of male and female stereotypes is complete. The active, aggressive, dominating boy has been formed, and so has the girl – submissive, passive and dominated. While the boy has been forced into a mould which not only permits but obliges him to act and realise himself as much as possible – if only in terms of competition, success and victory – the girl has been forced into an opposite direction: that of the non-realisation of the self. Because of this reductive conditioning, the largest part of the female's vital energy is suppressed and inhibited, then deviated towards unhealthy feminine masochism. According to Hélène Deutsch, this process is what engenders a so-called 'true femininity'. Women have destroyed their own creativity and hidden or mutilated their intelligence. They have imprisoned themselves in the misery of a daily repetition of paltry events and have destroyed themselves for the 'pleasure' of putting themselves at the service of men. Maximum security and protection are the false counterparts to what has been taken away from them. In exchange for renunciation and submission they have received only underdevelopment.

Conditioning is of course much more easily accomplished when the female in question has a physical constitution basically weak in vital energy. Since conditioning begins from the very first moments of life, it is only necessary to measure at this precise moment the quality and quantity of energy to be inhibited and deviated forever. I. Lézine shows,[7] in research which has already been cited,[8] that hypertonic girls – that is, those who tend to be wild, agitated, highly mobile, active and independent – preserve this temperament up to the age of four, which coincides with their introduction to nursery school. Often, though, they continue to be unruly within the home, at school they are capable of concentrating their attention and passing for timid and conscientious children. Psychological tests of their classroom behaviour reveal that they are inhibited, maniacal, and scrupulous. It is evident that for most of them the pressures of school are too painful because they come simultaneously from the teacher, the school structure itself, and from their peers. Furthermore, these pressures demand that the girls conform rapidly and completely to what is asked of them – to the point where the tension they experience is unbearable. The fact is that by the age of five, few girls have succeeded – if one can use such a word in this context – in being totally conditioned and have miraculously been able to preserve a good dose of energy, vitality, creativity, independence, autonomy, pride and dignity.

'When do you think I'll be big enough to go for walks all by myself?' asked a little girl, not yet four, who had followed me for a walk through woods near her home. 'It's so boring always to have to walk with grown-ups.' This remarkably intelligent child could still dream of solitary, adventurous walks. But for how much longer? How many little girls of the same age still have enough imagination, autonomy and vitality, enough of a need to affirm themselves, to see the future in terms of a conquest of the world around them? How many of them have been damaged by conditioning before such desires can even come to mind; damaged to the point that they no longer even experience any fascination for that adventure which is life?

Independence and creativity

By the time they are six and entering primary school, most little girls have lost their creativity. Few of them retain even a feeble trace of it, and these will still have to overcome the stumbling block of puberty, emotional encounter with the opposite sex and the dilemma which arises from it: self-realisation as an individual or submission to explicit demands for 'femininity' from men who will force them to restrain their creative personality from then on.

The multiple reasons for an absence of creativity in little girls can all be brought down to one. Their education forces them much more than boys into a state of dependency. This dependency is incompatible with creativity since the latter presupposes a strong dose of freedom in order to maintain itself and be productive.

Torrance writes, 'Creativity, by its very nature, requires both sensitivity and independence.' [8]

> Presently in American culture, but also in ours, sensibility is considered to be an exclusively 'feminine' characteristic, while independence is thought to be 'masculine'. Such value judgment creates one of the greatest social obstacles to the development of creativity. In effect, a creative young man seems 'sensitive' and thus effeminate in comparison to his peers; while girls sometimes have interests which are traditionally considered 'masculine', such as science or politics. This is why they often inhibit their 'creative process' to safeguard their 'masculinity' or 'femininity'. This, in part, also explains why women seem less creative than men. The pressure of social prejudices weighs more heavily on them. For instance, a girl who is interested in 'scientific' subjects or political problems often loses part of her charm in the eyes of male friends, while females find her 'eccentric'. Yet a conjunction of extreme sensitivity and an independence, which can break into rebellion, is a constant in such individuals not only before but during adolescence and adulthood.[9]

If sensitivity and independence are, as Torrance maintains, indispensable for creativity to manifest and realise itself, it then becomes impossible for most girls to maintain it. This is so precisely because their spontaneous striving for an independence equal to that of boys is broken once they enter an educational system whose principal objective is to make them dependent. Furthermore, they are continually driven to turn their attention away from political, intellectual, social and artistic problems in order to concern themselves with paltry, insignificant issues of a practical nature. This automatically limits their cultural horizon. To give free play to creativity, it is necessary to have sufficient access to the cultural heritage and to possess intellectual independence: the freedom to criticise, reject and detach oneself from received values in order to grapple with new ones. One must be strong.

> Creative persons have a well-developed autonomy of judgment; a tendency to non-conformism, a well-developed sense of humour, a great diversity of interests on the artistic and scientific level. On the other hand, they lack the 'normal' motivations vis-à-vis scholarly or professional success, which represents exactly what others expect of them.[10]

As opposed to this, dependency establishes strong links with the cultural values of the social milieu in which the person lives. It engenders unconditional and uncritical acceptance of these as well as the desire to possess to the maximum the qualities recognised by this milieu, and to conform to the demands of others. If a talent for the exact sciences is the sign of a 'masculine' intelligence, as M. Fattori states, and if this is not considered desirable in girls, they will forbid themselves such interests in order to conform to the qualities of their more 'feminine' peers and not be rejected or excluded by their group.

Adler states: 'There is a strong prejudice against little girls. They are often told that the female sex is not gifted in mathematics.[11] If a little girl's passion for the sciences is not an all-encompassing one, not only will she not attempt to compete with boys, but she will submissively lower herself to the level of incapacity of other girls of her own age. Only a small number, driven despite themselves by the force of their intelligence and desire, will persevere in this kind of 'masculine' field. But they will always be looked upon with suspicion and distrust. Instead of being accepted for their value, there will always be someone to ridicule them if they have not fully preserved their 'femininity'. They will not be given the respect usually accorded to high intelligence. They will be seen as abnormal exceptions, women who have 'a man's brain' or simply 'who have one'. Their intelligence, it will be said, and their desire to affirm themselves are the expression of their rivalry with men. If they are not pretty, it will be said that they have emphasised intelligence in order to compensate for their difficulty in attracting men. They will be accused of 'penis envy' and be called 'castrating females'. Guilty of the anomaly of being more intelligent than many males, they will be detested and avoided by men because they have committed the crucial error of not being 'objects'.

For a woman and even more so for a little or adolescent girl, imbecilic [12] criticism can easily provoke grave crises. As Simone de Beauvoir observes:

> For the young girl, on the contrary, there is a separation between her human condition, as such, and her feminine condition. What makes the young man's departure into life relatively easy is that his vocation as a human being and his vocation as a male are not opposed: his childhood has already predicted this happy fate. It has often been noted that from puberty onward, the young girl loses ground in intellectual and artistic domains. There are many reasons for this. One of the most common is that the adolescent girl does not meet with the encouragement which is given to her brothers. On the contrary, she must *also* be a *woman* and she is forced, in addition to professional duties, to take on the responsibilities implied by her femininity. In effect, it is not by increasing her human value that she will gain in male eyes; it is by modelling herself in accordance with masculine dreams. . . . To be feminine is to reveal oneself as impotent, futile, passive and docile.

And stupid! There is no place where girls are not constantly given confirmation of the fact that one prefers them stupid. (After that, one is of course quite free to reproach them for their stupidity.) Even when they display intelligence and curiosity, they are continually discouraged by the disinterest shown for their questions, by evasive, ambiguous, false, or approximate answers, if not by an explicit statement that these are not areas which should interest them. The classic line goes, 'You would do better to . . .' And what the little girl would be better off doing is, as if by chance, always something less important than what she would have liked to do.

'Dear Giovanna,' the editor of a children's magazine wrote in the letter column, in answer to a little girl of nine who asked why Romans, but not Greeks, had used vaulted arches in their architecture, 'You have asked a very intelligent question for a little girl.' He thus expressed a widely held opinion that little girls, being most often idiots, do not ask intelligent questions. And he proceeded to give a disappointing answer to a perfectly justified question.

For someone who has been programmed to be dominated, intelligence is a very embarrassing quality. Once it has manifested itself everything is done to discourage it so that there are no means for it to become conscious of itself. Instead the superiority of feminine intuition is exalted. For it suits the one who dominates to have his own desires understood even before they have been formulated – and satisfied by a person who has been formed to consider others' needs as more important than her own even when they run counter to her own.

This exalted feminine intuition is universally considered the 'natural' emanation of a being biologically destined for maternity and the education of children. Given this function she is said to be 'naturally' gifted with those powers of divination which will permit her to act towards them in the best possible way. But intuition is in reality the result of being conditioned to submission and the related necessity of constantly having to take into account the ideas, moods, reactions and desires of those who dominate. Allport says,[13]

> Their rôle as women demands that from the youngest age, they learn to be sensitive to the needs and behaviour of others. . . . In a society where a double moral standard still exists it is wise for a woman to take into account the character of her friends and to be circumspect on their behalf.

It is precisely this enforced circumspection – this permanent necessity to consider what others think and expect, what it is proper to do or change, the right amount to ask for something with a chance of success, to interpret the significance of others' features, expressions and gestures – which will determine a woman's own deportment. This circumspection is the origin of that famed feminine intuition and it uses up a great deal of energy which could be otherwise deployed. Intuition is a typical defensive characteristic in oppressed people. The proof of this lies in the fact that men who are in difficult situations which demand that they foresee the reaction or moods of others – as for example in prison – also develop 'intuition'.

It is true that women, by nature of their condition, are obliged to develop their intuition. Since this quality has affirmed itself, they choose to go into professions which require it. This is a process which follows the law of functional autonomy, as defined by Allport.

Discrimination continues: A look at primary and secondary schools

Where little girls are concerned, primary school teachers confirm the observations made by nursery school teachers. Girls are conscientious to the point of obsession. Their notebooks are tidy. There is not a stain on them, not a fingerprint or doodle. The letters forming the words are straight, show no hesitation, are excessively legible and so light that they testify to the absence of strength which characterises these girls. Their essays are well composed: just long enough not to disappoint the teacher. Their content is completely conformist. Concepts of the beautiful, the good and the bad abound. If a position must be taken up they are always on the side of the good and show contempt for the bad. Banality is evident in every line. A homage to authority always takes first place. The whole is bathed in a sticky romanticism, replete with sugary descriptions, sentimentality, improbable landscapes and situations. The girls' compositions parallel their behaviour. They are full of an anxiety to appear perfect and the desire to surprise teachers and friends with fine sentiments displayed in a tone which has nothing spontaneous about it.

The boys' notebooks are quite a different story. Dirty, crumpled, torn, they are the visible witnesses of those daily gestures in which school bag, notebooks and accessories are hurled any way. Disorder seems to be the rule here as far as the insides of the notebooks are concerned. Consistent characteristics include scratched out words, stains, mistakes, fingermarks, words on top of words or cut in half, letters upside down, non-existent or fanciful punctuation, undotted i's, a total lack of organisation in the use of the page and an absence of even the most rudimentary aesthetic principles. But these notebooks, as tattered and messy as they have grown because of the boys' direct and intense participation in life outside the school (since *he* does have an extra-scholastic life), are full of vitality, invention and imagination, even if chaotic and disorderly.

The boys' compositions are always shorter than the teacher asked for. Ideas are hurriedly expressed, without any concession to a good style or indeed grammar and spelling. The judgments are peremptory, often even contradictory. Poetic descriptions are rare and if they exist one senses that the first person not to take them seriously is the author himself. While the girls produce drawings which are well-proportioned and graceful, the boys create more vulgar passionate sketches, devoid of proportion and grace. Colour obeys impulse rather than reflexion and the tints defy the outlines: red fields and meadows, green suns, distorted houses, disproportionately sized people. The drawing will often creep off the page (without the least aesthetic preoccupation) and invade a nearby dictation or piece of homework. These are wild adventurous note-books, as free as their owners.

Little girls apparently do better in the first years of primary school. There is no teacher who can resist the attraction of a well-ordered exercise book which answers to her personal 'feminine' conception of order. The girls' notebooks elicit praise. They seem to be the refined products of exquisite sensibilities, but are in reality the fruits of creativity extinguished forever which has given way to a melancholy conformism.

Little girls are always attentive. They listen to every word the teacher utters. They never forget their pen or exercise book at home. They always have a sheet of paper or eraser to lend out and do so in a way which will elicit the greatest possible attention from others. They understand everything, remember everything. They sit immobile and well-behaved at their desks, knees and feet pressed together. They are annoyed by the boys' noise and are ready to beg them to be quiet if they are prevented from hearing the teacher's words. Tension devours them and the desire for approval agonizes them. What passes for natural calm is really savage self-discipline and a tensely, nervous attention aimed at grasping what may be expected of them, even before it is expressed. There is none of the boys' solidarity amongst the girls. They gossip, tell tales, spy on each other and report back to the teacher. Their behaviour has all the characteristics of an oppressed group.

Separation of the sexes, so much part of nursery school, con-tinues at the primary level. The result is evident: girls and boys are completely strange to one another and are often enemies. Nevertheless, few battles erupt between them, despite the violence which might be done. Injustices, real or imagined, are reported to the teacher who often judges their content less than the manner in which they are reported. To her, it seems quite normal that boys persecute little girls and behave aggressively towards them. She may reprimand undue aggression and ask them to be 'nicer', but she will equally tell the little girls to be less 'of a nuisance'.

To uphold that it would be better to keep boys and girls apart completely from primary school onwards merely re-emphasises their inability to live together. This has been caused by a difference in upbringing so acute that it has made it difficult for them to find common ground. The solution is not to separate them because they are different and can harm each other. Rather it lies in abolishing this difference by bringing them up as individuals and not as members of one or another sex.

Little girls 'like their teacher more' or at least they take pains to tell her so and demonstrate it to her. They want to kiss her. They bring her flowers or a little gift. They make a drawing for her. They are ready to do things for her with an unmeasured pleasure and pride which appears on their eager-to-please faces. They will abandon their work at any time to pick up the teacher's pen, to put the sugar wrapper into the bin when she has her morning coffee, to open the door for the occasional departing visitor, or to get up and greet any person who enters.

Their greatest ambition seems to be to place themselves at the beck and call of any person who represents authority. They are already prepared to prostitute their glances in order to receive a smile from the other person. They always smile, but laugh very little, while boys do the opposite. They are servile and have little pride.

Just as in nursery school, when the teacher asks that the room be tidied, it is the girls who hurry to do it. Boys continue their tactic of doing things badly and unwillingly so that the teacher asks less and less of them. Girls display a perfect efficiency. No teacher could prevent herself from complimenting them. But it is just such praise which weakens even further the consciousness they have of their own value as individuals. It puts the emphasis, as always, on their function as persons whose principal duty it is to be useful to others.

One would think that boys might be humiliated by their daily confrontation with the courage, zeal and efficiency of little girls. But this rarely happens. Boys have a thousand ways of constantly reassuring themselves of their value as men. Furthermore most teachers even while they admit that girls are 'easier to deal with, quieter and more docile' will end up by saying that 'boys give one more satisfaction'. They explain this apparent contradiction by emphasising boys' greater creative potential. If girls tend to reproduce what is proposed to them, then boys, on the contrary, tend to introduce variations, propose solutions, discuss and invent. All this is considered to be more dynamic.

The introduction of an obligatory school leaving age has not essentially altered the fact that more girls than boys will discontinue their studies after the end of primary school to take care of the home or go out to work. The school leaving age has merely been pushed forward by a few years. Even now more girls than boys stop after their fourth year at secondary school.

If there are only girls in a family, it is easy to allow all of them to continue their studies. If the family consists of boys and girls, unless it is particularly well off, the boys will be urged to pursue their studies to the detriment of the girls. Often, too, a school of an inferior calibre is chosen for the girls.

The discrimination between boys and girls continues at secondary school level. Apart from the psychology of secondary school teachers (women for the most part) [14] who like primary and nursery school teachers continue to demand that students conform to accepted values, secondary school institutes discrimination in its very rules and regulations. Girls, for example, are more often required to wear a particular uniform – in our case the traditional humiliating black smock – while boys wear whatever they please. Tilde Giani Gallino,[15] professor of Latin, reports the reasons why the teachers in her establishment voted unanimously against abolishing a uniform for girls. (Boys cease to wear one after primary school.) These reasons are moral and repressive ones, put forward by people who do not see girls as individuals, but simply as sexual objects who could awaken boys' desires.

Gym classes are given separately to both sexes. This is done to ensure that exercises are found which are suitable to the specific 'nature' of each sex: strength in boys, grace in girls. However, one also sees in this separation the fear of promiscuity which might be awakened from the moment that lighter clothes are necessary.

Discrimination however reaches its peak in the organisation of technical studies. Courses here are clearly divided into male and female kinds of work. They are given by men for boys and women for the girls and mixed classes are separated.

Government educational handbooks present a clear line as to what these courses should contain: [16]

> Without establishing rigid limitations, those courses which are particularly well suited to boys – not only because of their *nature*, but also because of their *interests* – will consist of work which transforms currently used raw materials (wood, metals, plastics etc. . . .) into finished products. For girls more suitable work will be that which consists of furnishing, gardening, horticulture and flower-growing.

As opposed to other disciplines, the content of these courses is left up to teacher's own initiative. The female teachers, who generally come from women's technical colleges, are for the most part experts in home economics. For them, their own background provides the only possible one. The anachronistic schools from which they come condition them from the first as to what activities the pupils can engage in.

The male 'technical studies' teachers have more varied backgrounds. They are often architects, engineers, experts in public works, agriculture or industry. The link between teachers' backgrounds and the guidelines set down in government proposals bears the desired fruit. Girls spend hours in needlework classes doing embroidery, crocheting and not much else. To top it all off, the results of this handwork are among the most useless and frustrating. Boys, on the contrary, learn to use tools, do carpentry and minor electrical work. This might be time wasted for both sexes, but the fact is that the girls look upon the boys' 'technical studies' with envy. They sense that they are judged incapable of even such modest feats and that they have been reduced to humiliating needlework. Furthermore, the boys look with contempt upon their pursuits. As always, the two sexes find themselves in antagonistic positions. What is suited to each has been decided beforehand. Both male and female have been prevented from freely choosing the activities which they might prefer as individuals.

Aware of the complete uselessness of such activities, one particular school attempted to institute more stimulating tasks to be carried out during technical study periods. For the boys an attractive laboratory was fitted out. For the girls, who were still quite little, there had been talk of installing a cradle, a small bath, and a baby's changing table in one corner of the room, so that they could practise baby-care. One teacher pointed out that this kind of discrimination in the activities offered to students was altogether prejudicial and that the choice among all possible activities should be left to them. The headmaster and the teaching staff, after having calmly reflected on the problem, and after having admitted that it deserved thought, nevertheless concluded that the girls must be made to understand that it would be 'for their own good' if they avoided putting themselves in embarrassing and ridiculous situations. Thus they should be kindly advised to take the courses dealing with baby-care and not the others. It was unnecessary to explain anything to the boys, since it was assumed that none of them would show the least interest in baby-care.

This paternalist and well-meaning suggestion constitutes one of those arguments which carries a great deal of weight. It makes it quite clear that the girl who does not choose 'baby-care' but rather a more 'masculine' study is displaying an abnormal tendency in relation to the accepted model. What girl would have the courage – at an age where one is painfully seeking one's own identity and often conforming at great personal cost to feminine stereotypes – to make such a 'deviant' and non-conformist choice? Authentic aspirations can easily be snuffed out by pressures of this kind.

A technical studies teacher in a special school where separation of courses had been avoided and boys and girls could and were indeed encouraged to choose whatever activity they wished, reported that when he had proposed a series of welding exercises, out of 54 pupils who had elected this activity, 36 were girls. The same teacher, however, admitted that when the pupils had decided to construct a large sailboat – which meant sawing the wood and preparing the sails – he himself had suggested to them that they divide the work according to their various abilities. To the girls he confided the task of sewing the sails. For their part, the girls had recourse to the boys when they wanted to change the used blades of the electric saw. This had seemed quite appropriate to the teacher and had relieved him from having to understand that it might have been better, once and for all, to teach girls how to change blades and boys how to use a sewing machine.

During my final year of pedagogical training, I had the opportunity of getting a sample of opinions from female technical studies teachers on the discrimination which resulted from putting boys and girls into separate classes, and on the various activities engaged in during these classes. The problem was raised by one of the teachers participating in the training programme. She disagreed with the opinion of one of the professors, a young woman who gave courses in home economics and who believed that division between the sexes was necessary since men and women were different and had 'by nature' different interests. This opinion was unanimously approved by the group of teachers.

They were all women between twenty-five and fifty years of age and they agreed that 'feminine grace' had to be protected; that it was the teachers' duty to make sure that girls' behaviour conformed to such principles; that their scrupulous attention was directed at making sure that girls 'don't feel ill at ease in their own skin and in life' and that all this was 'for their own good'.

The principle at the basis of this matter – is it fair to discrimin-

ate between the activities of young people on the basis of sex? –
was avoided by referring to government guidelines which of course
anticipated such discrimination. It was as if government pro-
grammes represented the essence of truth and justice and could not
be subject to criticism in order to be revised.

One realised that women were incapable of seeing in the matter
at hand a discriminatory and thus unjust act which contributed to
malforming the consciousness of young people. As in many other
similar instances, these women were defending conservative positions to the detriment of their own sex.

Notes

1 Irenaus Eibl-Eibesfeldt, op. cit.
2 In *Vita dell'infanzia*, no. 7, April 1972.
3 B. Linner, 'What does Equality between the Sexes Imply?'. Essay
   presented to the annual congress of the American Orthopsychiatric
   Association, Washington, D.C. 1971.
4 Margaret Mead, op. cit., pp. 318–319.
5 Grazia Honegger Fresco, 'I bisogni della prima eta nelle case dei
   bambini', *La via feminile*, no. 1, December 1968.
6 *Vita dell'infanzia*, no. 7, April 1972.
7 Odette Brunet and Irene Lezine, op. cit., p. 155.
8 Paul E. Torrance, *Guiding Creative Talent*, Prentice-Hall Inc.,
   Englewood Cliffs, 1962.
9 Marta Fattori, op. cit., p. 40.
10 Ibid., p. 39.
11 Alfred Adler, *The Problem Child*, Putnam, New York 1963.
12 Simone de Beauvoir, op. cit.
13 Gordon W. Allport, op. cit.
14 For an analysis of the opinions of primary school teachers see
    Mario Barbagli and Marcello Dei, *Le vestali della classe media*,
    Il Mulino, Bologna 1969.
15 Tilde Giani Gallino, op. cit.
16 Ministry of Public Education, *Orari e programmi d'insegnamento
    per la scuola media statale*, State Polygraphic Institute, Rome 1963.

CLASSROOMS OF RESISTANCE

Chris Searle

In a school in Poplar during the last two years, Chris Searle has been attempting to 'develop through imaginative writing, the generous, empathetic and fraternal instincts' of the children he teaches. The Chile coup, the South African miners' strike, Ulster, the Flixborough disaster, and nearer home, the opening of the £8,000,000 Tower Hotel on the site of the old St. Katherine's dock to mention but a few, are events which are discussed in the classroom. From these discussions come the children's poetry, prose and drama contained in this book. It is illustrated throughout with photographs and line drawings.

It is in the children's work that the ideology of Searle's teaching is powerfully revealed: he believes that Education is only valid if it contributes to liberating all mankind, and that his teaching must further 'the knowledge of resistance to, and organisation against exploitation and subjection, and contact and empathy with the oppressed of the world'.

The Writers and Readers Publishing Cooperative

was formed in the autumn of 1974.

We are a cooperative collectively owned and operated by its worker-members, several of whom are writers.

We are members of the Industrial Common Ownership Movement.

Our policy is to encourage writers to assume greater control over the production of their own books; and teachers, booksellers and readers generally to engage in a more active relationship with publisher and writer.

We attempt to keep our overheads as low as possible so as to keep our book prices down, and thereby benefiting readers.

We welcome response which will tell us what readers wish to read.

If you would like to be put on our mailing list and receive regular information about our books, please write to:

Writers and Readers Publishing Cooperative
25 Nassington Road London NW3
175 Fifth Avenue New York. NY 10010